For Paul

THE TRIAL OF TEMPEL ANNEKE

THE TRIAL OF

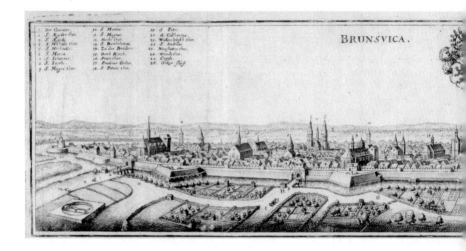

BRUNSVICA.

TEMPEL ANNEKE

Records of a Witchcraft Trial in Brunswick, Germany, 1663

Edited by Peter Morton

Translated by Barbara Dähms

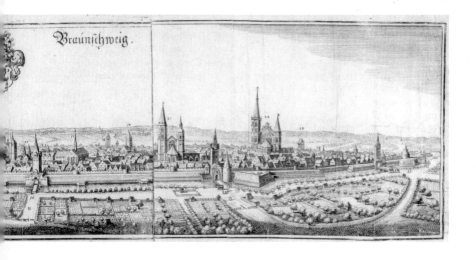

University of Toronto Press

First edition published by Broadview Press 2006.

LIBRARY AND ARCHIVES CANADA CATALOGUING IN PUBLICATION

   The trial of Tempel Anneke : records of a witchcraft trial in Brunswick, Germany, 1663 /edited by Peter A. Morton ; translated by Barbara Dähms.
Includes bibliographical references and index.
ISBN 978-1-55111-706-5
1. Roleffes, Anna, ca. 1600-1663 – Trials, litigation, etc. 2. Trials (Witchcraft) – Germany – Braunschweig. I. Morton, Peter Alan II. Dähms, Barbara, 1954-

KK270.7.R65T75 2005   345.43'59760288   C2005-905905-2

We welcome comments and suggestions regarding any aspect of our publications—please feel free to contact us at news@utphighereducation.com or visit our internet site at www.utphighereducation.com.

North America
5201 Dufferin Street
North York, Ontario, Canada, M3H 5T8

2250 Military Road
Tonawanda, New York, USA, 14150

ORDERS PHONE: 1-800-565-9523
ORDERS FAX: 1-800-221-9985
ORDERS EMAIL: utpbooks@utpress.utoronto.ca

UK, Ireland, and continental Europe
Plymbridge Distributors Ltd.
Estover Road, Plymouth, PL6 7PY, UK
TEL: 44 (0) 1752 202301
FAX ORDER LINE: 44 (0) 1752 202333
orders@nbninternational.com

The University of Toronto Press acknowledges the financial support for its publishing activities of the Government of Canada through the Book Publishing Industry Development Program (BPIDP).

Book design and composition by George Kirkpatrick

Printed in Canada

Figure 1 (previous page) Cityscape of Brunswick from the east 1652 by Merian after Conrad Buno 1641. This engraving shows the city as it appeared at the time of the trial. The municipality of Hagen, where the trial took place, is on the right side of the cityscape.

Contents

Preface

This book is a translation of the records of a witchcraft trial that took place in Brunswick, Germany, in 1663. Our intent has been to make the complete contents of the original documents available in English, as they exist in the archive, and occasionally as they can be reconstructed from other sources. Our decision to translate the records arose from our joint belief that they offer an unusually close picture of the people involved, especially of Tempel Anneke herself. Of the trial records in the Brunswick area that we have read, including some as detailed as the Tempel Anneke case, this one stands out in its vividness.

The book is organized into three basic parts. In the Introduction, we give some historical background and describe the legal context of the trial. The trial records and supplementary archival documents make up the bulk of the book. In the last section, we have included appendices to assist with the Latin terms used in the records, and with the identification of the herbs and medicinal ingredients mentioned in the trial testimony.

The introduction provides background to the trial's social and historical context. The first section outlines the situation in Brunswick at the time of the trial, and presents some key historical background: we detail here the early modern "composite" nature of witchcraft as consisting of both *maleficium* and diabolism, and also the role of the Carolina (the criminal code of the Holy Roman Empire) in the actual structure of the legal proceedings. The second section of the Introduction describes the archival documents: of what they consist, who wrote them, and the positions and responsibilities of the court officials named. This second section also considers some aspects of the translation, such as the choice of specific words as well as certain conventions we have adopted in reproducing the text.

We wish to emphasize what this volume does not undertake to do. It is intended as a primary source document, with as much background information as is needed to make sense of the text. In this light, the introductory chapter is not in any way intended as a general introduction to the history of the witch trials of early modern Europe. The general history of the trials is a large and complex subject, embracing a number of controversial issues, and we have not attempted a synopsis of it here. For those readers with an interest in the wider history of the witch trials, we have included footnotes with references, and a brief section of further readings. Here again, because the literature is so vast, we have included in this section only those materials that offer an introduction to the topic, rather than attempting any kind of general bibliography.

We have not included our own interpretation of the records or provided a synopsis of their contents. While we certainly have our own theories about the trial, we do not want these to come between the reader and the text. We adopted the same approach in the translation. In the interests of providing as direct an experience with the records as possible, this is a fairly literal translation which preserves the style and character of the original, while leaving the result easily readable in English.

A note to the Second Printing:
In addition to the correction of some minor errors, we have added a new entry to the Supplementary Civic Records: Record 4. Testimony from the trial of Lücke Behrens for witchcraft, Brunswick 1672. This record contains a description of the arrest of Tempel Anneke at the home of Christian Loers.

Acknowledgements

First of all we thank Katharina Dähms and Hans-Dietrich Dähms for their support and hospitality during research visits to Brunswick. We thank the Department of Humanities of Mount Royal College for continuous support and encouragement. For much advice and direction with sources and historical material, we thank Peter's departmental colleagues: Tom Brown, David Clemis, Steven Engler, Debra Jensen, and Scott Murray. Manuel Mertin, Dean of Arts of Mount Royal College, has also been supportive of the project from the outset.

The project received financial support, as well as encouragement, from the Scholarly Pursuits Committee of Mount Royal College. Professor J.J. MacIntosh of the University of Calgary was enthusiastically helpful in obtaining financial assistance.

The staff of the *Stadtarchiv Braunschweig*, especially Herr Krone and Herr Nickel, have been continuously helpful, both during our initial collecting of documents and with the selection and reproduction of illustrations. We also thank the *Landesmuseum Braunschweig*, and specifically Herr Otte, for help with illustrations.

Janet Sisson of Mount Royal College was most helpful with the Latin translations. We received much good advice and some useful references from three anonymous reviewers.

Finally, we thank Mical Moser of Broadview Press for her encouragement and patience, as well as her constant good humour.

List of Illustrations

List of Maps

Introduction

I. Historical Background

Sometime in June of 1663 Anna Roleffes, known locally as Tempel Anneke, of the village of Harxbüttel[1] near the city of Brunswick, was arrested on suspicion of witchcraft and was imprisoned in the municipality of Hagen in Brunswick.[2] The earliest written allegations against her appeared in the summer of 1662, and from these records it seems that there were already at that time official enquiries into her activities. Her ultimate arrest stemmed from the charge that she used sorcery to obtain the return of goods stolen from a roofer, Hans Tiehmann. Following her arrest the court investigated a number of other allegations against Tempel Anneke, some from many years earlier, and numerous witnesses were questioned about their knowledge of her affairs. The trial lasted from 25 June to 30 December. Under torture she confessed to witchcraft, and on the latter date she was beheaded and her body was burned.

At the time of her trial Tempel Anneke was a widow, living on the farm of her son, in Harxbüttel, a small village some seven kilometers northwest of Brunswick. Her husband, Hans Kage, had been killed in 1641. In her first testimony before the court Tempel Anneke says that she was born in Harxbüttel, and that she was five years old when Duke Heinrich besieged the city in 1605. The name, Tempel Anneke, derived from the fact that a church property, called the Tempel Hof, of the Order of St. Blasius in Brunswick, had been established in the village. A public house was part of the property, and the publican at the time of the trial, Hans Harves, was called "Tempel Hans." We do not know how Anna Roleffes obtained the same name. "Anneke" is a diminutive of "Anna."

The trial testimony indicates that Tempel Anneke practiced as a healer and diviner (a person who can obtain hidden information such as the location of lost goods). She had business in Hagen, and the testimony of her activities originates from several towns and villages in the area northwest of the city. Many of the common social characteristics of those accused of witchcraft at the time apply to Tempel Anneke. She was female, elderly, widowed, and

---

1 The name of the village has a form common to the region: the term "büttel" is from the ancient Saxon word for house or farm, to which is added the name of the original family. In this case the family name was originally "Harckes." So the name indicates the farm of the Harckes family.

2 For a description of Tempel Anneke's arrest in Hagen, see Document 4 of the Supplementary Records.

dependent upon her family. She may have portrayed her practice as involving magic, although she denies this in her earliest statements to the court. She was literate and owned a few books and herbals, which was unusual for a farm woman of the time. In her testimony she claims to have gained her first medical knowledge from her mother, who had been a maid to a barber in her youth. (In the seventeenth century barbers provided basic medical services in addition to cutting hair.) She claims to have obtained additional knowledge from her books, and from the practices of shepherds and other local people.

A. The city of Brunswick in the seventeenth century[1]

Brunswick lies in the eastern region of Lower Saxony in northern Germany, between Hannover and Berlin. In the twelfth century the Guelph duke, Henry the Lion, selected Brunswick as his principal residence, and he built there a castle and a large cathedral, the Dom of St. Blasius. Over the centuries Brunswick became an important commercial centre, strategically located on principal trade routes between northern European cities. In the seventeenth century it was a fortified city of some 15,000 inhabitants. Until 1671 Brunswick belonged to the Hanseatic League of cities, whose members were independent in commerce and local governance from their surrounding jurisdictions.

At the time Brunswick had an unusual civic structure, and to an extent this affected the trial's legal structure and proceedings. From its earliest days as a settlement on the banks of the Oker River, the city was formed of distinct and largely independent municipalities or boroughs. By the seventeenth century there were five such municipalities: Altstadt, Hagen, Neustadt, Sack, and Altewieck. Each had its own town hall, mayors and town council, court, and (except Sack) its own district church. There were in addition two independent ecclesiastical districts: the cathedral chapter of St. Blasius in the city centre, and the church and monastery of St. Aegidien in the south. For important matters of common concern the city maintained a General Council, the *Gemeine Rat*, comprised of representatives of the individual municipal councils.

The seventeenth century was a harsh time for much of central Europe, and the trial took place during a particularly difficult period in Brunswick's

---

1   For the history of Brunswick in the seventeenth century, we have drawn on Jarck and Schildt (2000), Monderhack (1997), and especially Spiess (1966).

history. An important line of the Guelph dukes, the house of Brunswick-Lüneburg, had its seat in the town of Wolfenbüttel, just 15 kilometres south of Brunswick, and for a long time the dukes had claimed their right over the city. They besieged the city several times, and blocked its trade routes for long periods: not surprisingly, this had a serious impact on the local economy. The dukes gained full control of the city in 1671, and it became part of the duchy of Brunswick-Lüneburg. A much larger military engagement, the Thirty Years War, raged around Brunswick between 1618 and 1648. The war had a devastating effect on the civilian population. Tempel Anneke's husband was killed by soldiers outside of Wolfenbüttel in 1641. Through the skillful diplomacy of its officials, Brunswick managed to avoid besiegement, unlike many cities in the region. Its success in avoiding the conflict, however, brought with it a different cost. As an island of relative peace, the city was swamped with refugees, both noble and poor, especially from nearby Magdeburg (which was burned to the ground in 1631). The resultant overcrowding brought disease, and exacerbated outbreaks of the plague. To add to these difficulties, the region suffered a series of unusually cold winters. Ironically, the frigid winter of 1657/58 brought to an end the worst plague of the century, in which more than 5,000 people in the city died.

Figure 2 The Brunswick Opera House (formerly the Municipal Hall of Hagen) Copper Plate by Beck 1747. This is an illustration of the Municipal Hall of Hagen, where much of the trial took place, as it appeared in 1747. By this date the building had been converted to an opera house. Unfortunately it no longer exists.

Figure 3 Cityscape of Brunswick from the east by Merian after Conrad Buno 1641 (detail). This is an enlargement of Figure 1, showing the municipality of Hagen. The church on the left side, labeled with the number 20, is St. Catharine's, the district church of Hagen. Directly behind the church were the Hagen Market and the Hagen Municipal Hall. The Wenden Gate, where the execution took place, is on the right side of the picture. Wenden Street, along which Tempel Anneke was taken for execution, runs from St. Catharine's to the Wenden Gate, between St. Andreas church (number 22) and the city wall.

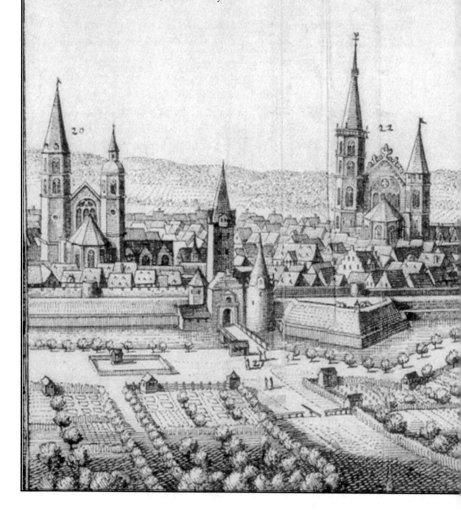

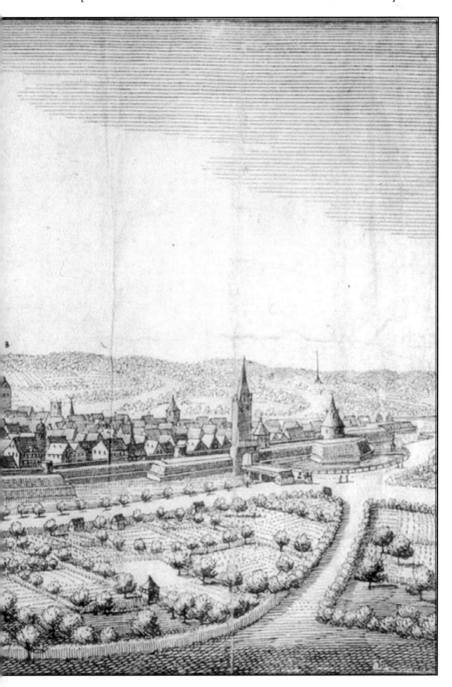

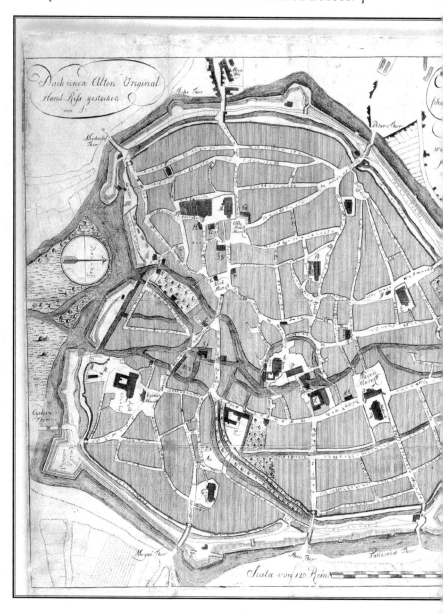

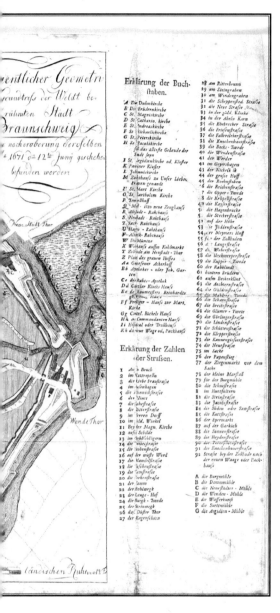

Map 1 Plan of the City of Brunswick 1671. This plan was commissioned shortly after the occupation of the city by the Dukes of Brunswick-Lüneburg in 1671. The plan is oriented to the east, so that north is on the right. The moat around the city is the Oker River. The Dom of St. Blasius and the castle square appear in the centre of the plan, labeled "A." The Hagen Market, labeled Hagen Marckt, is below and to the right of the castle square.

Map 2 Plan of the City of Brunswick 1671 (detail). This is an enlargement of Map
1, showing the municipality of Hagen in more detail. The municipal hall of Hagen
is just in front of St. Catharine's church, which is labeled "D" on the plan. Fallersleben Street, where the magistrates took testimony, runs east–west on the right side

Wende Thor

of the church. The Wenden Gate (labeled Wende Thor) is clearly marked on the right side of the plan. Wenden Street is the large thoroughfare between the Hagen Market and the Wenden Gate. Kaiser Street, in Neustadt, where several events in the trial took place, is next to St. Andreas church at the top.

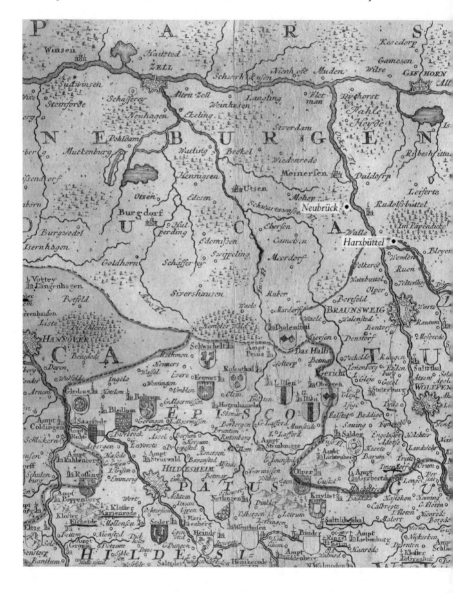

Map 3 District of the Duchy of Brunswick 1715 (detail). This is a detail from a map of the duchy that shows the areas around the city in which the trial events took place. Brunswick is in the centre, and the Oker River runs through the centre of the map from south to north. As Harxbüttel does not appear on this map, we have added it beside the Schunter River northwest of Brunswick. We have also added Neubrück, where a good deal of testimony was collected. Gifhorn is at the top of the map, and Campen is northeast of Harxbüttel. Lehre is just below Campen and to the right. Wolfenbüttel, where Tempel Anneke's husband was killed, is the fortified town to the south of Brunswick.

B. Perceptions of witchcraft in the seventeenth century

The trial of Tempel Anneke is a single instance of a much larger episode in European history: the so-called "witch-hunt of early modern Europe," which lasted from the middle of the fifteenth century through the first half of the eighteenth century. During these three centuries thousands of people were executed for the crime of witchcraft.[1] The proliferation of witchcraft trials was in part a result of the linking together of two very different understandings of witchcraft—"*maleficium*" and "diabolism." To understand the context of Tempel Anneke's trial, we must explore the context of both *maleficium* and diabolism, as well as how they were brought together in early modern legal understanding.

The first conception of witchcraft is that of harmful magic or sorcery. (We will use "magic" and "sorcery" interchangeably.[2]) The Latin term for harmful magic in the Middle Ages and early modern Europe is *maleficium*. Although it is difficult to define precisely, in this context we can describe magic as the use of extraordinary powers within objects, words, and signs, to achieve some practical end. "Extraordinary" powers does not imply what today we would think of as "supernatural," in the sense of existing outside the natural order altogether. In medieval and early modern Europe, the tools of the sorcerer were thought to be part of God's natural creation and bounded by its laws, and hence "magic" was thought to rely on powers within the realm of nature. Magical powers are more correctly described as "preternatural," that is, as part of the natural world created by God yet outside the ordinary course of nature.

We can see something of a continuum between what we might call "high magic" and "low magic."[3] At one end of the continuum, we can identify as high magic those practices involving sophisticated arts practiced by people with some degree of education. Two examples of such high magic are the arts of alchemy (the transmutation of metals) and necromancy (the raising

---

1   It is difficult to determine precisely the total number of executions. Newer research rejects early speculation of hundreds of thousands or even millions, and puts the figure at less than one hundred thousand. The most recent survey for continental Europe is Monter (2002). For an idea of the geographical extent of the witch trials, see also the maps at the front of Briggs (1996).

2   This is not always reliable. For example, Kieckhefer (1989) restricts the term "sorcery" to the misuse of medical or protective magic. We have preferred to use "sorcery" interchangeably with "magic" because it is the best translation of *Zauberey* in the trial records.

3   See Levack (1995, pp. 7–8)

of spirits and demons). At the other end of the continuum, low magic is the use of simple spells, charms, and rituals, by people without formal training or education. In medieval and early modern Europe, many forms of low magic—for healing and divination, among numerous other purposes—were passed on between generations or drawn from individual experience.[1]

Both high and low magic could be used for either benevolent or malevolent ends. Fear of harmful low magic was common in villages and towns in this period, and this fear was one of the factors leading to the proliferation of witch trials. Trials often began with accusations of *maleficium* within a community. When people suffered unusual losses or injuries, they frequently looked to their neighbours for the cause. For example, people with magical abilities were believed to be able to kill livestock, to cause human illness, death, and impotence, to prevent a mother's milk from flowing, and to bring hailstorms to destroy their neighbours' crops.

Accusations of *maleficium* by themselves, however, would not have yielded the large numbers of trials and executions that occurred between 1450 and 1750. The second component of witchcraft (which was necessary to instigate a witch-hunt), was the belief that people guilty of *maleficium* acquire their powers through a pact with the Devil. In this pact, witches were believed to abandon God and to give themselves, body and soul, to the Devil. The term for worship of, or subservience to, the Devil is "diabolism." In return for their allegiance, the Devil was believed to grant witches the power to perform magic. In the eyes of theologians and the courts of law it was the pact with the Devil—rather than *maleficium*—that was the real crime of witchcraft. Diabolism is a crime of apostasy—the renunciation of God and the holy sacraments.

The belief that magicians acquire their powers through a pact with the Devil was well established among theologians in medieval Europe. This assertion had been made as early as the fifth century by Augustine.[2] In the thirteenth century Thomas Aquinas argued that all forms of magic involving signs or symbols require the aid of demons, on the grounds that the signs are powerless in themselves.[3] The practice of necromancy, which spread in

---

1 There were many forms of magic between the two extremes. For an introduction to magic in the Middle Ages and the Renaissance, see Kieckhefer (1989), Jolly (2001), and Peters (2001). A classic study of magic in early modern England is Thomas (1971).
2 See the translations from Augustine in Kors and Peters (2001, pp. 43–46).
3 See the translations from the writings of Thomas Aquinas in Kors and Peters (2001, pp. 87–104).

the late Middle Ages, was condemned in the fourteenth century by inquisitors of the Church, who argued that the magicians could not command the demons as they claimed, but instead offered them worship.[1] In the fifteenth century, the belief that magic requires a pact with the Devil was also applied to those accused of harmful low magic.[2] People accused of *maleficium* by their neighbours came to be seen as devil worshippers and apostates. Thus the two quite distinct ideas—*maleficium* and diabolism—became linked, forming a composite notion of the witch as harmful sorcerer and agent of the Devil. The linking of diabolism to *maleficium* provided the grounds upon which accusations of witchcraft, arising from the general population, led the legal authorities to conduct investigations and prosecutions.

This composite allowed the crime to be perceived differently by the legal authorities—jurists and judges—than it was by the witnesses and accusers. It was believed by demonologists and jurists that a witch's magic is completely ineffective without the aid of the Devil. They argued that the Devil deceives the witches into believing that their spells and charms work to bring about their ends, whereas in fact the effect is produced entirely by him.[3] Thus the witch's purpose is incidental to the real crime of apostasy. It made no difference to the guilt of the accused whether the magic was intended for good or for ill. This view was not always shared by the witnesses and the general population. The accusations of witnesses in Tempel Anneke's trial make no reference to a pact with the Devil, and include only the harmful effects that her magic was believed to produce. Her neighbours were frequently willing to hire her for her magical abilities without concern about the Devil at all.

The complex understanding of witchcraft that developed during the fifteenth century was promulgated by a large number of books and treatises on the threat and nature of witchcraft, which were subsequently used in sermons and legal tracts. Among the earliest and most well known of the witchcraft treatises is the *Malleus Maleficarum* (*The Witch's Hammer*) of 1487 by the Dominican inquisitor, Heinrich Kramer,[4] but dozens of similar books were printed and re-printed throughout the early modern period. A later book that also had a large impact is *De la démonomanie des sorciers* (*On the*

---

1   See, for example, the translations from Nicholas Eymeric's *Directorium Inquisitorium* of 1376 in Kors and Peters (2001, pp. 120–26).

2   For a discussion of what may have prompted this link, see Levack (1995, pp. 36–37), and also Kieckhefer (1976).

3   On the subject of the inefficacy of magic and witchcraft without the aid of the Devil, see Clark (1991).

4   See Summers (1928).

Demon-Mania of Witches) by Jean Bodin (1580/2001). Bodin's work was used by jurists at the University of Helmstedt, who served as legal advisors to courts of law in the region of Brunswick and beyond.[1]

Based on this composite understanding of witchcraft, certain practices and signs of witches could be expected of the accused. Witches were believed to travel at night to gatherings, called sabbaths, where the Devil would be present. There they were thought to engage in an orgy of blasphemous and immoral rites, including cooking and eating infants, and mocking Christian ritual.[2] Satan was also imagined to force unnatural sex on his witches, although the act was supposedly cold and unpleasant. Witches were believed to give homage to the Devil in disgusting ways, such as kissing his behind while he appeared as a goat. Once a witch had agreed to a pact with Satan he placed a secret sign on her body, and an unusual mark on the body of the accused was often taken as proof of guilt.[3]

Gender played a key role in the medieval and early modern understanding of witchcraft. Although the percentages varied from region to region, a significant majority of those accused were women. In addition to the statistical facts about the trials, the demonological literature of the time argued that women are particularly susceptible to witchcraft. A standardized list of beliefs about women, in support of this conclusion, recurs through the literature. Women are of weak understanding, and are hence more likely to be ensnared by the lies and illusions of the Devil. Their supposed sexual appetite leads them to consort with demons. For example, in a now infamous passage of the *Malleus Maleficarum*, Kramer writes that, "All witchcraft comes from carnal lust, which in women is insatiable."[4] Many other attributes were added to the list, including curiosity, vanity, and greed. The issues surrounding the relations between gender and witchcraft have been the subject of considerable debate,[5] and research into both early modern perceptions of gender, as

---

1 Kauertz 2001, pp. 90–91.

2 The origin of belief in a devil-worshipping society has a complex history. On this subject, see Cohn (1993). On the subject of witchcraft as the inversion of Christianity, see Clark (1997, pp. 1–134).

3 Not all regions of Europe accepted this complex concept of witchcraft with equal conviction. In England, for example, belief in the sabbath never fully took hold. Moreover, the different understandings of aspects of witchcraft were subjects of learned debate throughout the period of the witch trials. See Clark (1997, pp. 149–311).

4 See Summers (1928, p. 47).

5 For an introduction to some of the issues, see the Introduction and articles in Volume 4, Gender and Witchcraft, of Levack (2001). On the specific topic of old women and witchcraft in Germany, see Rowlands (2001), which includes a discussion of recent literature on gender and age in the witch trials.

well as the position of women in society at that time provides key insights into our understanding of witch trials.

This period has been described as the "witch-craze" as a result of the many terrible abuses of justice: this term was first popularized by Trevor-Roper in 1967. Yet it is important to recognize that the demonologists and jurists involved in the witch trials were not victims of any kind of collective irrationality. Clark (1997) has shown clearly that issues such as the nature of magic, the powers of the Devil, and the prosecution of witchcraft were the subjects of extensive scientific, legal, and theological investigation across Europe. Kauertz's (2001) study of the University of Helmstedt, mentioned above, reveals that debates about the nature of witchcraft and its prosecution were carried out across the three faculties of theology, law, and medicine.

We end this section on a cautionary note. The nature of the trials varied from one time and region of Europe to another. Issues such as the use of torture, the relative independence of local jurisdictions, and the judicial procedures in effect, all had an impact on the numbers of trials and the likelihood of execution. Differences of opinion among theologians, jurists, scientists, and judges, as well as differences in attitudes and belief among the local people, all contributed to the complexity and variety of people's experiences. The trial of Tempel Anneke is a single instance of a complex phenomenon, and it is as much influenced by local factors as it is by the general concept of witchcraft.

C. The trial of Tempel Anneke

Witchcraft was a capital offence, punishable by death. In Brunswick, all criminal trials were overseen by the Higher Court of the city, an office of the General Council, rather than the municipal courts, which handled civil cases. In criminal trials, both the decision to prosecute and the final judgment were made by the Higher Court. The investigation and examination of witnesses were carried out by the Lower Courts of the respective municipalities.

Despite the fact that the charges against Tempel Anneke match the features commonly found in the witch-hunt, some of the worst abuses of justice that occurred during the period are not found in the trial. Witch-hunts were occasionally brisk and brutal with large numbers of people tried and executed. Torture was sometimes indescribably cruel, and was often used to coerce the accused into naming other people with whom they had associated or had seen at the sabbath.[1] The execution of convicted witches was occasionally an act of wanton cruelty rather than the carrying out of a court sentence.[2]

The Brunswick region was not free of large witch-hunts. Heinrich Julius, Duke of Brunswick-Lüneburg from 1564 to 1613, a devout Lutheran and Bishop of Halberstadt, executed many witches from across the duchy, with a particularly high number between the years 1590 to 1594. A chronicle of the time reports that he often burned "10, 12 or more" witches in a single day and that there were so many stakes at the place of execution that the site "looked like a little forest."[3] In a Constitution directed at the clergy of Brunswick he castigates the clergy for "looking through their fingers" at witchcraft and other sins.[4] August the Younger, Duke of Brunswick-Lüneburg from 1635 to 1666 and founder of the magnificent library that still bears his name, was also zealous in the prosecution of witches. Around the year 1610, before his succession to the dukedom, he is known to have burned 70 witches in the small town of Hitzacker.

The features of large witch-hunts are not found in the action against Tempel Anneke. The procedure follows the common practices in criminal investigations, and the use of torture and the execution are carried out according to the decisions of the General Council and the standard legal practices of the time. One of the earliest documents, dated August 1662, mentions that Tempel Anneke might have been aware of the fact that investigations were being conducted into her activities. Since the arrest and trial proper do not begin until the following year, we can infer that the authorities were slow to commence legal action. The records indicate that the court was diligent in gathering witnesses and acquiring testimony, and there are places where they were concerned that Tempel Anneke's confessions are not sincere (although most likely, the concern was related to the legal validity of the confession rather than its truth). Finally, although she was questioned about other people with whom she associated or from whom she learned her witchcraft, the court did not press her to implicate others. There is no evidence of any follow-up investigations.

---

1 The trials at Ellwagen, described in Midelfort (1972, pp. 98–112), provide an example of such a witch-hunt in which large numbers of people were tried and executed.

2 See for example Kunze (1987).

3 Rehtmeier and Bünting 1722, Vol. 2, p. 1099.

4 Heinrich Julius 1593.

D. The Carolina[1]

During the period of the witch trials, the German lands were part of the Holy Roman Empire. Although politically the region fell under the authority of the Emperor and the Reichstag, which passed legislation for the empire, in fact the region was highly decentralized. In particular, the courts of the various jurisdictions operated largely independently of centralized control.[2] There was, however, an imperial criminal code, The Criminal Court Regulation of Emperor Charles V, known as the Carolina.[3] The Carolina was intended to impose order, and some degree of control, over the jurisdictions throughout the Empire. Among the issues it addresses are the orderly collection of testimony and evidence, their careful recording, and consultation with legal experts in cases of uncertainty. The latter stipulation was heavily emphasized because trials within the Empire were often conducted by local authorities with little or no legal training. In Brunswick at the time of Tempel Anneke's trial it was required that all judgments concerning capital offences be reached in accordance with the Carolina, as well as the local city regulations and the traditional Saxon laws of the region. (For local civic regulations, see "Additional Civic Records" below.) The Carolina was the major influence on the actual procedures through which the trial progressed.

The distribution of the Carolina was an important step in changing the role of the courts from adjudicating private accusations and disputes—the so-called accusatorial model—to initiating and conducting criminal investigations. The model upon which the Carolina is based was developed by the medieval church from Roman origins, and is now referred to as the inquisitorial model. Although the distinction between accusatorial and inquisitorial trials is not always clear, the distinguishing feature of inquisitorial trials is that the investigation—the identification and summoning of witness, for example—is directed by the court rather than the parties involved.

The principal parts of criminal investigations under the Carolina were the testimony of reliable witnesses and interrogations of the accused. In es-

---

1   In the following comments we draw on Langbein (1974). For an introduction to the legal contexts of the witch trials generally, see Levack (1995, pp. 68–99).

2   It is argued by Levack (1995) and Monter (2002) that the lack of central control over local courts was a contributing factor in the large numbers of trials in the German lands of the Empire. This is perhaps illustrated by the witch-hunts in the duchy of Brunswick-Lüneburg.

3   See Schroeder (2000). Much of the Carolina is translated into English in Langbein (1974, pp. 261–308).

tablishing the guilt of the accused the Carolina relies heavily on confession, although it also allows a guilty verdict when two reliable eyewitnesses are available. When the weight of preliminary testimony sufficiently indicates a guilty verdict, the threat of torture and then torture itself is specified in order to obtain a confession. It is important to recognize that torture was a regular part of criminal trials in Germany at the time, and was not reserved especially for those suspected of witchcraft. Nonetheless, since witches were believed to be agents of the Devil, a threat of extraordinary power, the usual safeguards against abuses of justice were often ignored. Some legal experts considered witchcraft to be a *crimen exceptum*, an exceptional crime, wherein the ordinary rules of justice had to be relaxed.

There are several distinct stages in trial procedure as outlined in the Carolina. The first was the initiation of investigation. In cases of judicial prosecution a decision must be taken that there exists sufficient suspicion of criminal activity to warrant investigation. Here the Carolina stipulates investigation into someone who is "suspected of a crime through common repute, or is notorious on account of other credible indication."[1]

Once the investigation is initiated, the second and perhaps most important stage is the collection of testimony to determine whether there is what the Carolina calls "legally sufficient indication" to proceed to torture. Sufficient indication meant that the evidence collected during the investigation shows a strong enough presumption of guilt that the court should proceed to obtain a confession, by torture if necessary. Twenty-six sections of the Carolina are devoted to illustrating the circumstances that constitute such indication for crimes of various sorts. One of these stipulations applies to people suspected of sorcery:

> When someone offers to impart sorcery to other people, or threatens to bewitch someone and such befalls the threatened person, and the aforesaid person otherwise has associated with men or women sorcerers, or has employed suspicious things, gestures, words, and signs such as characterize sorcery, and when, further, the said person has a bad repute of similar sort, then that constitutes a legally sufficient indication of sorcery and is adequate basis upon which to examine under torture. (Article 44, translated by Langbein 1974, p. 279)

---

1   Article 6, translated by Langbein 1974, p. 269. This part of the trial of Tempel Anneke is found in Document A through Folio 4.

In the trial of Tempel Anneke this stage is documented in Folios 5 through 23, and constitutes the largest part of the trial proceedings.

If sufficient indication is established, the court is then instructed to seek a confession, first through the threat of torture and, if necessary, through torture. In the trial of Tempel Anneke the advice to proceed to this stage, received from the legal faculty of the University of Jena, is found in Folio 24. The Carolina does not lay out rules governing the severity of the torture used, but rather the function that the torture should perform. The intent should not be merely to coerce the accused into a confession, but to obtain further information upon which a judgment could be based. Thus, for example, judges are warned against the use of leading questions, and are instructed to use torture to obtain information from the accused "which no innocent person can know." Article 52 of the Carolina describes the information that should be sought from those who confess to sorcery.

> When someone confesses to sorcery, he shall also be questioned about the causes and circumstances (as above), and moreover, with what, how, and when the sorcery occurred—with what words or deeds. Further, when the person examined states that he hid or held on to something which allegedly facilitated the said sorcery, then afterwards there shall be an attempt to find it; when, however, the said sorcery was committed with other things through word or deed, then they too shall be investigated to see whether they are infected with sorcery. The person shall also be asked from whom he learned such sorcery, and how it came about; whether he also employed such sorcery against more people, and against whom, and what damage thus occurred. (Article 52, translated by Langbein 1974, p. 281)

To be valid, a confession obtained under torture must be confirmed by a repetition of the same confession without torture (albeit under the threat of resumed torture if the accused should recant). If the accused should withstand all of the torture—which became increasingly severe—without confessing, he or she was commonly spared execution. However, those who did not confess were often banished from the city, which was not a light sentence for the poor or elderly.[1] Upon completion of the attempt to obtain a confession,

---

1   This was the fate, for example, of Lücke Behrens in Brunswick in 1671 (Brunswick City Archive C V 101). She was tried by some of the same court officials as was Tempel Anneke. However, she survived

the trial proceedings were presented for the final judgment of the court.

Some of the influence of the Carolina on trial procedures within the Empire derived from its insistence on the consultation of legal experts in forming judgments. In Brunswick after 1615, as in many other German jurisdictions, the trial documents in every case of a capital offence were forwarded to the legal faculty of a respected university for a legal judgment, called a *Gutachten*. In the trial of Tempel Anneke the testimony was forwarded to the University of Jena. The *Gutachten* received from Jena stipulates death by fire, which is the sentence specified in Section 109 of the Carolina.[1] The court in Brunswick, however, did not consider itself formally bound to follow the *Gutachten* of the universities. Rather they served only as part of the grounds on which the final decision was taken. On the basis of Tempel Anneke's contrition, the sentence of death by fire was commuted by the court to beheading and burning of the body.[2]

The final stage of the trial was the recording of a formal confession, called the *Urgicht*, and the subsequent carrying out of the sentence. Prior to execution, however, the Carolina gives careful instructions for a final hearing, the so-called *Rechtstag*. This hearing was purely ceremonial. Although it included submissions to the court and the consideration of evidence, the final decision of the court had already been made. In cases where a full confession was available, it was read out before the court. The *Rechtstag* was held just prior to the execution, which in Hagen would have taken place outside the Wenden Gate.

II. Understanding the Text

The trial of Tempel Anneke was long and complex, lasting seven months and including testimony from a broad spectrum of witnesses from numerous

---

severe torture without confessing, and was banished from the city. An attempt by her husband to lift the banishment was resisted by local people in Hagen.

1   Section 109 reads,

Someone who harms or disadvantages people through sorcery should be punished from life to death, and one should do this punishment with fire. But where someone uses sorcery and hasn't harmed anyone with it, he should be punished otherwise, according to the circumstances of the case, in which the judges should use guidance, as is written below concerning the seeking of guidance. [Our translation]

2   The severity of the punishment needs to be seen in the context of the time. For example, the Carolina gives death by fire as the appropriate punishment for arson, and premeditated murder was punished by death on the wheel. Beheading was the penalty for serious theft.

jurisdictions, as well as frequent questioning of Tempel Anneke herself. Full records were kept of every deposition and testimony, as well as correspondence with surrounding jurisdictions. As a result, the written record of the trial is extensive and detailed.

A. The archival source

The records from which the translation is drawn come almost entirely from a single file in the city archive of Brunswick. In the seventeenth century full records of trials were not always preserved, and often only the final judgment was kept in the public record. The complete record of the trial of Tempel Anneke, however, was preserved and was placed in the city archive in the early nineteenth century.[1]

The archival record consists of some 210 pages, originally divided into 45 folios, which document the trial in chronological order. Each folio has a cover page with the folio number, the date, and a description of the contents. In our translation we have placed these covers at the beginning of each folio. There are three sets of documents that do not fit the chronological pattern. All three date from before the arrest of Tempel Anneke and the trial proper. First, Folio 17 contains the earliest record in the file concerning Tempel Anneke, dated August 17, 1662. The next oldest document of testimony against Tempel Anneke is filed as part of Folio 15. The latter two documents were written in the jurisdiction of Neubrück, near Harxbüttel, and it is likely that they were filed on that basis, rather than according to their chronological order. Finally, the third oldest document in the collection was simply inserted at the back of the file without a folio number. This is dated April 9, 1663, and it contains the first record of Tempel Anneke's dealings with the roofer, Hans Tiehmann. It is from this incident that the formal charges against her originated. Since these three documents do not have folio numbers in the same chronological order as the rest of the record, we have placed them at the beginning of the records in chronological order, and labelled them Documents A, B, and C respectively.

A few important documents originally in the file are now missing, but fortunately most of the missing material has been recorded elsewhere. Folios 1, 2, and 3 are no longer in the collection. Folio 1 contained the record of the first interrogation of witnesses against Tempel Anneke. There are summaries

---

1 Brunswick City Archive H V 250.

of the contents of this folio in Görges and Spehr (1892, pp. 421–30) and Wrampelmeyer (1910). Unfortunately, neither is very reliable; in our translation we have formed a composite of what is found in both summaries.[1] Of Folios 2 and 3 only the title page of Folio 3 is preserved in the file. Folio 2 contains the questions first put to Tempel Anneke, and Folio 3 has her answers to them. However, Rohmann (1983) contains excerpts from the trial records, and this includes the contents of these two folios. Folio 24, the first of two letters written by the faculty of law at the University of Jena to the court in Brunswick, has also disappeared from the collection. The title page of this letter is reproduced in Rohmann, and the content is transcribed in Görges and Speyer, and in Wrampelmeyer. Finally, the last page of Folio 45, Tempel Anneke's final confession, is missing, but it is also reproduced in Rohmann.

There is one feature of the trial against Tempel Anneke that strikes the modern reader as especially odd. The questions that were put to the accused were formed in accordance with the stipulations in the Carolina, and each was written *before* the actual questioning and thus without the benefit of the answers to previous questions. This was common practice at the time. The curious result is that questions often stand in contradiction to answers given earlier. Tempel Anneke is often asked how and from whom she learned to do something that she has just denied doing at all. Most often her answers to such questions are simply silence. In the original records the questions to be asked of the accused are listed in one folio, and the answers without questions are recorded in the following and later folios. In our translation we have repeated the questions with the answers, since otherwise the records are difficult to read.

B. The court officers[2]

The trial of Tempel Anneke was carried out under the authority of the General Council of the city of Brunswick. Among its duties the General

---

1 Both Görges and Spehr, and Wrampelmeyer, include in Folio 1 details that only emerge later in the trial, and moreover these details are different in the two summaries. For this reason we have translated only those items common to both summaries. Incidentally, both of these works state that Tempel Anneke was the last person tried for witchcraft in Brunswick, an assertion repeated by Rohmann (1983). However, the complete records exist of two subsequent trials in the city, one against Elizabeth Lorentz in 1667 (Brunswick City Archive B IV 15b 32), and another against Lücke Behrens in 1671 (Brunswick City Archive C V 101). Rhamm (1882, pp. 79–80) refers to the trial of Katharina Sommermeyer in 1698.

2 The contents of this section are largely drawn from Spiess (1954, 1966, and 1970).

Council served as the Higher Court of the city, charged with the administration of, and final judgment in, all capital offences. Trials of the Higher Court were held in the municipal hall of Hagen, illustrated in Figure 6. (Rohmann 1983, p 13).

A senior judge (called a *Syndicus*) of the Higher Court was the highest civil servant, and was trained in law. A lower judge was called a *Consiliar*. The initial order to carry out the investigation, recorded in Folio 4, is signed by Johann Strauch, the first *Syndicus*. The final judgment of the court was written by Johann Burchard Baumgarten, the second *Syndicus*. His statement of the final judgment of the Council is Folio 44, which is reproduced in Figures 7 and 8.

The officers conducting the actual investigation were members of the Lower Court. The permanent members of the Lower Court were two magistrates (*Vogt*), salaried civil servants drawn from the two largest municipalities, Altstadt and Hagen. In the trial of Tempel Anneke these are Otto Theune, magistrate of the municipality of Hagen, and Johann Velhagen, magistrate of the municipality of Altstadt. The Lower Court also held ten members of the General Council, two from each municipality, called a *Gerichtsherr*, which we have translated loosely as "Court Officer." In the trial of Tempel Anneke the two officers of the court for the municipality of Hagen are Hennig Blome, General Council member for the guild of butchers, and Gabriel Oeding, General Council member for the guild of tailors. The scribe of the Lower Court was Johann Pilgram, who is the draftsman of most of the documents in the trial records. The city executioner was Hans Pfefferkorn, who was also responsible for conducting the torture.

Folio 23 contains a letter from Dr. Laurentius Gieseler, the *Stadtphysicus*, whom we would now describe as chief medical officer of the city. The *Stadtphysicus* was among the highest and best-paid officers of the city, appointed directly by the Council. He held authority over all medical practice in the city, including the overseeing of physicians and barber-surgeons, and the regulation of apothecaries and bath-houses. The letter in the trial records was requested by the court to determine that the medicinal ingredients used by Tempel Anneke could not have the effect that she claimed for them without the aid of magic.

The trial records also contain letters to and from officers in the towns and jurisdictions outside the city. The officials in these jurisdictions were officers of the ducal courts, with the title *Amtmann*, translated in our text simply as "civil officer." The following civil officers are named in the records:

Martin Bregen, officer of Gifhorn

Johann Damm, officer of Campen

Johann Gürn, officer of Neubrück

Andreas Schonberg, regional civil administrator (*Landhauptmann*) of Gifhorn.

There is one last set of court officers, the bailiffs (*Fronbote*). Their responsibilities included carrying communications between jurisdictions, performing arrests, and the incarceration of prisoners. The city employed quite a number of bailiffs for communication with officers in the neighbouring towns, which is evident in the letters between Hagen and the surrounding jurisdictions of Neubrück, Campen, and Gifhorn.

One aspect of the letters between the jurisdictions merits a word of explanation. The letters begin with very elaborate formal addresses, which are sometimes repeated in the body of the letter. For example, in Folio 10 the court in Brunswick addresses the civil officer in Gifhorn with the sentence, "Our greetings and service in friendship first, high-born, powerful, strong also knightly, admired and learned, especially highly honoured gentleman and reliable friend." The name given to this form of address is Chancellery Style (*Kanzleistil*). Each term carried a specific meaning in terms of the rank or position of the officials addressed, so that the formal addresses served the function of acknowledging the respective levels of authority. There are two words, *Veste* and *Ehrenveste*, which pose a problem for translation. The term *Veste* originally designated a fortification, and from this origin the two terms were used in the sixteenth century as forms of address for minor nobility. In the trial records, however, the terms indicate officers of courts with given levels of authority. Since no similar terms exists in English, we have translated them by "strong" and "knightly," which are at least close in the literal meaning.

C. The Supplementary Civic Records

Following the trial records, we have included in our translation a section from the local civic regulations concerning sorcery, and some items drawn from the accounting books of the court. Record 1, the civic regulations, indicates the kinds of sorcery that are punishable within the city and the penalties for them. The accounting records document the amounts paid to the officers of the court involved in the trial of Tempel Anneke. Record 2 includes the salaries paid to the court officials. The first account lists the administrative salaries of the judges. There are four entries included here: the salary of the professor of law at Jena who served as legal expert to the city, the salaries of the two *Syndici*, Johann Strauch and Johann Baumgarten, and the salary of the *Consiliar* or lower judge. The second of the accounts lists the annual base salaries of the permanent officers of the Lower Court, who conducted the interrogation and questioning of witnesses. There are four individuals listed in this account: the two magistrates (Otto Theune and Johann Velhagen), the scribe (Johann Pilgram), and the executioner (Hans Pfefferkorn). Record 3 contains items drawn from the "Books of Prisoners" of 1663 and 1664. These contain supplementary amounts paid to the bailiffs, to the priests who accompanied Tempel Anneke to her execution, bills for wine for the mayors and officials who attended the execution, and the money paid to Hans Pfefferkorn, the executioner.

D. Currency[1]

In seventeenth-century Brunswick there were two distinct ways of counting money. In the early Middle Ages the only coin that was in common use in Brunswick was the Pfennig (abbreviated as *Pf* or *d*). For calculating larger sums the values, Schilling (β) and Mark (*mr*), were used. The latter were not coins but merely amounts used in calculation. The Schilling was equivalent to 12*Pf*, and the Mark was equivalent to 20β (= 240*Pf*). Despite the later introduction of new coinage, these medieval values remained in use as units of accounting well into the seventeenth century. Hence, the fines levied by the courts, the salaries paid to court officials, and the amounts paid for services, are recorded in Pfennig, Schillings, and Marks.

In the fifteenth and sixteenth centuries two additional coins were introduced: the Groschen (*g* or *gr*) and Taler (*Tal*). The Groschen was worth 12*Pf*, and the Taler was worth 24*g* (= 288*Pf*). By the seventeenth century the general population no longer referred to the Schilling and Mark, but only to the coins. Thus in the witnesses's testimony Pfennig, Groschen, and Taler are mentioned in amounts paid or received. There are two additional coins mentioned in the witnesses's testimony: the Ortstaler and Mariengroschen (*mg*). The Ortstaler was a quarter Taler (= 6*g*), and the Mariengroschen was ⅔ of a Groschen (= 8*Pf*). In one of the episodes documented (particularly

---

1   The information in this section comes largely from Spiess (1966, pp. 548–52).

in Folio 11) the Count of Lehre is said to have lost six ducats, a gold coin of large value.

E. The language of witchcraft

Elements of the early modern understanding of witchcraft or magic can be further highlighted by a brief exploration of the words used in the trial records to describe Tempel Anneke's activities. The modern German words for a witch and for witchcraft, *Hexe* and *Hexerei*, were relatively recent at the time of Tempel Anneke's trial. An older word, *Zwickersche*, is used once in Document C. Although *Hexe* and *Hexerei* are used in the trial records, much more common are the words based on the verb *zaubern*. The noun, *Zauberei*, can be translated as either "magic" or as "sorcery." We have used "sorcery" wherever possible. Tempel Anneke is most often described as a *Zauberin* or a *Zaubersche*, which translate neatly as "sorceress." The verb *zaubern* does not translate easily into English, since grammatically it can take a direct or indirect object. We have translated it as "conjure." Finally, there is the verb *bezaubern*, which can only be translated as "bewitch": this is unfortunate, because the records also use the word *behexen*, which is also translated as "bewitch."

There are other aspects of the language that are more subtle. Acts of witchcraft are often described in the documents as involving "sending" living beings into the bodies of the victims. At the time there was a common belief in northern Germany that these beings were little creatures, called *Holden*.[1] Witches were believed to send (*weisen*) these into their victims to cause lameness or illness. Rhamm (1882, p. 13) has the following description from a document in the town of Quedlinburg in 1575: "... small things, not very tall, they wear red things like linen, a face like a large half nut, small, small hands like a little worm, and with blue lights in them...."[2] In the trial of Tempel Anneke *Holden* are not anywhere described in detail, yet some of the language preserves this idea. For example in Folio 2 this question is posed: "Whether she didn't conjure the evil things into the head of Jürgen Roleffes?" In Folio 28 Tempel Anneke says that she had taken three "things" from the body of Heinrich Cordes's son and sent them into a calf because "they had to eat." The sense in which magic was accomplished by "sending things" is also

---

[1] The term originally meant a good or friendly spirit. (See e.g. Lexer 1885/1992.)

[2] "... kleine Dinger, eine Spanne hoch, haben rothes Zeug an wie Hareß, Angesicht wie eine halbe Nuß und kleine, kleine Hände als ein Meddell, und blaue Lichtlein darrinen." Quoted from *Zeitschrift des Harzvereins für Geschichte V* p. 91.

used without the direct reference to a particular object or creature. Thus, in Folio 18 Tempel Anneke is asked whether "it had been sent to the farm of his brother Jürgen Rollefes" and whether she wanted to "send it out again."

Tempel Anneke is also accused of what we have translated as "divining." The German verb, *nachweisen*, is less direct, meaning more generally "point out," "show," or "indicate." It is clear from the way in which the word is used, however, that an illicit or magical ability is referred to, hence our choice of translation.

There are occasionally descriptions of forms of witchcraft caused directly by the Devil. As with the *Holden*, the Devil himself sometimes flies into a person's body (*hinein fahren*) to cause injury or illness. He also whispers (*zublasen*) information to people. In Folio 29 there is a phrase in which Satan is said to "blow into" (*einblasen*) Tempel Anneke, which we have translated as "incite."

There is one further form of magic that is worth noting. Tempel Anneke is accused of being able to "lock and unlock," which refers to the ability to cause and remove impotence. This is a very common accusation made against witches, both by the general population and by demonologists.[1] Schütte (1907, p. 134) has a description of the common belief in Brunswick at the time.

> Normally it occurs during copulation, that someone who wants to take away the possibility of continuation of the line from a young married couple secretly carries a lock in their pocket, closes it, and throws it into water. If it isn't then found and opened, it was believed that the marriage of the couple will remain childless.

Rhamm describes the same practice in the region, and adds that it was also common to tie knots into string to achieve the same effect.[2]

F. Notes on the translation

The grammar, spelling, and use of upper- and lower-case letters, are very irregular in the original documents, a common feature of written texts during this time. Also, the quality of the prose varies greatly, sometimes very clear and other times very crude. We have attempted a translation that preserves as much as possible the character of the original. A common grammatical feature

---

1 See, for example, the descriptions in Summers (1928, 54–58 and 117–18).
2 1882, p. 14.

is the use of commas where modern writers use full stops. The result is that the testimony is largely a string of run-on sentences. We have preserved this wherever it does not thoroughly confuse the English syntax. Capitalization and grammar are more difficult, since modern German and English are different in any case. We have had to put most sentence structure into modern English form, especially the position of subordinate clauses, so that some of the convoluted grammar of the original is lost. We hope, though, that the result preserves something of the distinctive character of the original. There are two aspects of the writing that could not be preserved. One is the regular use of the conjunctive tense in German to indicate something reported but not confirmed by the speaker. The other is that in the past perfect tense the auxiliary verb (e.g. "has" or "is") is frequently omitted.

We have adopted the following conventions in our translation.

- We have left Latin phrases in the original. This is done to preserve as much of the character of the original documents as possible. The Latin is often irregular and Germanized. Sentences and terms used only once are translated in footnotes, and Appendix A contains translations of the frequently repeated Latin phrases.

- We have used a single spelling for the names of people. The original documents use a variety of spellings for most names, since spelling at the time was not standardized. For the purposes of the index and cross-referencing, we have chosen a single spelling for each name.

- We have used the modern spellings of town names to allow for easy recognition.

- There are three styles used for women's names. At the time in Germany women kept the last name of their father after marriage, rather than taking the name of their husband. Tempel Anneke, for example, is Anna Roleffes, although her husband was Hans Kage. However, women are also referred to by the feminine form of their husband's last name, with the endings "*se*" or "*sche*" or "*ische*." For example, Dorothea Mehrdorff, the wife of Hans Henkelmann, is also referred to as "the *Henkelmannische*." Finally, women are referred to by the feminine form of either their own profession or that of her husband. For example, Tempel Anneke is referred to as "the *Zaubersche*," and the baker's wife is referred to as "the *Beckersche*." We have left women's names in their original form wherever possible.

- The scribe uses the symbols /: ... :/ for indicating comments of his own inserted into the record of testimony. This was a common practice in this period, and we have retained these symbols in the text, with the scribe's insertions in italics.

- In repeating questions from earlier testimony we have sometimes added names to the pronouns to remind the reader of the person being spoken of. When we do this, we have put the name in square editorial brackets, [...].

- There are three different ways of referring to the months of the year, which we have preserved in the translation, as follows:

  1. in German, which we have translated directly into English

  2. in Latin for June, July, and August, ending with the genitive endings either "*i*" or "*ii*." Thus
     Juni or *Junii* = "of June"
     Juli or *Julii* = "of July"
     Augusti or *Augustii* = "of August."

  3. using the Latin words for the numbers seven through ten for the months September through December, with the genitive ending "*bris.*" Thus,
     7 in Latin is *septem* so that 7bris (*Septembris*) = "of September"
     8 in Latin is *octo* so that 8bris (*Octobris*) = "of October"
     9 in Latin is *novem* so that 9bris (*Novembris*) = "of November"
     10 in Latin is *decem* so that 10bris (*Decembris*) = "of December"

- As much as possible we have preserved the frequent use of hendiadin—repetitions of the same idea with different words—which occur frequently in the text. An example of a hendiadys is in Folio 6: "tossed or threw the aforementioned piece from an old shirt."

- The two terms, *Heilige Geist* and *Böse Geist*, can be translated either as Holy Ghost and Evil Ghost, or as Holy Spirit and Evil Spirit. We have used the latter.

[xlii]

- There are occasionally words that are illegible and phrases that are cut off the page, and we have indicated these with {...}. We have removed the court scribe's own self-corrections in most places; however, we retain these for interest in Folio 33 with an explanatory note.

One last comment on the trial documents: there are two people named Hennig Roleffes. The one most frequently mentioned is a resident of Wenden, near Harxbüttel, who charged Tempel Anneke with witchcraft and gives testimony several times. The other is Tempel Anneke's brother, of Harxbüttel. He was dead prior to the trial, but is mentioned in the records, in Folios 18, 28, and 29.

And, finally, a note on pronunciation: several words in the trial records have a vowel with an *umlaut*: *ä*, *ö*, or *ü*. The effect of an *umlaut* is to soften the vowel sound. The result is similar to placing an "e" after the vowel, as *ae*, *oe*, or *ue*.

Suggestions for Further Reading

Here we suggest some introductory readings for those interested in the broader history of the witch trials of early modern Europe. This is in no sense a general bibliography, but rather an indication of some starting points for those who wish to explore the topic further.

For those encountering the European witch-hunt for the first time, Levack (1995) provides a broad introductory survey of the witch-hunt as a whole, including its legal, intellectual, and social backgrounds. A good companion to this book is Kors and Peters (2001), which contains excerpts from historical documents, from early theological writings on magic to the end of the witch trials. *Witchcraft and Magic in Europe*, edited by Bengt Ankarloo and Stuart Clark, is a six-volume series of articles written especially for the series by specialists in various fields. The most relevant volume for readers of the Tempel Anneke trial is Ankarloo and Clark (2002). In this volume Monter (2002) and Ankarloo (2002) survey the most recent research on the witch trials on the continent and in northern Europe respectively, and Clark (2002) discusses the positions of witchcraft and magic in early modern culture.

There are two general bibliographies intended for the non-specialist: Levack (1995, pp. 261–269), and Briggs (1996, pp. 431–440). Both of these give the reader an overview of the literature up to the date of publication, organized by general topic, and also give some idea of the general perspectives on the issues surrounding the witch trials. Also useful, Levack (2001) is a six-volume anthology, which contains reprints of articles drawn from journals and anthologies on various aspects of the early modern European witch trials. For readers of the Tempel Anneke trial the volumes of most immediate relevance are Volume 1 (*Demonology, Religion, and Witchcraft*), Volume 2 (*Witchcraft in Continental Europe*), Volume 4 (*Gender and Witchcraft*), and Volume 5 (*Witchcraft, Healing, and Popular Diseases*).

On the subject of witchcraft trials in Germany, the following are available in English. Midelfort (1972) is a classic study of the witch trials in southwestern Germany. Behringer (1987/1997) examines the witchcraft trials and their political context in Bavaria. Two books by Lyndal Roper (1994 and 2004) examine witch trials in Augsburg and southern Germany from a psychoanalytic perspective. Rowlands (2003) is a study of trials in Rothenburg ob der Tauber that examines why trials there led to only one execution in ninety years, focussing closely on the narratives revealed in the trial records.

These studies, however, are of regions in southern Germany, which were different in various respects from north Germany and the Brunswick region. Studies in German that include the Brunswick region specifically are Rhamm (1882), Schütte (1907), Schormann (1977), and Lehrmann (1997).

There are some other works that provide useful comparisons to the trial of Tempel Anneke. Briggs (1996) draws extensively on the trial records in Lorraine in southwestern France, a region that experienced a large number of trials. His work focuses on patterns of accusation among neighbours and the responses of local authorities. His observations provide a good comparison to the accusations against Tempel Anneke. Kunze (1989) is a study of a single witchcraft trial in southern Germany that provides a striking contrast to the trial of Tempel Anneke.

The Trial of Tempel Anneke (1663)

Document A

[This document records the first known accusations of witchcraft against Tempel Anneke. It was originally filed as Folio 17, but it has been moved here because of its date. The testimony was given in Neubrück, outside of Brunswick, in August, 1662. For a description of the archival material that we are naming Documents A through C, see pp. pp. xxxiv-xxxv of the Introduction.]

Extractus Protocolli[1]
How Tempel Anneke brought a suit against Hennig Roleffes of Wenden, concerning his accusation of witchcraft against her, but, when they were supposed to be confronted with each other, she failed to appear.

Neubrück on the 28th of Aug. 1662

Actum[2] in the civic office of Neubrück
The 28th of August *Anno*[3] 1662

An old woman, called Tempel Anneke, from Harxbüttel appeared here, and the complainant reports, on what grounds does Hennig Roleffes from Wenden dare to impute witchcraft to her. Because she was innocent of that, she demanded the accused Roleffes be summoned and it be required of him that he make amends to her. In wanting justice for the plaintiff, it was promised to the same, that the accused would be summoned to appear before the office in eight days, where she could also appear again at the same time to await further judicial information. And in spite of the mentioned Hennig Roleffes appearing here on the specified day, Tempel Anneke nevertheless failed to appear, and her complaint made here is not pursued. Nor did she even come within the sovereign jurisdiction of this office, especially as the same might have found out that there are careful enquiries into what different kinds of suspicious business in Thune and Wenden, as well as elsewhere, what many evils she had both accomplished and started.

---

1   Extract from the record. For translations of Latin expressions see the glossary in Appendix A, pp. 158–61.
2   Legal proceeding.
3   In the year.

Document B

[Like Document A, this document was recorded in Neubrück and indicates official interest in Tempel Anneke prior to her arrest in June, 1663. Originally it was filed as part of Folio 15, but it has been moved here on the basis of its date.]

Extract Protocolli
What Master Heinrich Cordes, carpenter from Wenden, stated without torture at Neubrück, the 4th 7bris[1] 1662.

Ex protocollo[2]
Neubrück, the 4th 7bris 1662

When summoned, Master Heinrich Cordes appeared, and the same stated that 9 years ago he had an assistant named Stoffel Jürgens living in his house, and how this fellow was friends with Temple Anneke, she had often talked to him. Among other things, on one occasion the woman came, and with the fellow Stoffel Jürgens drank herself silly in his house. On that occasion she came to him, Heinrich Cordes, at his bed, and said there was a mandrake[3] present in his house, which wanted to leave him. But if he gave her half a Taler, it wouldn't do such a thing, because she could make it so that it would have to stay. When now said Cordes didn't want to hear her words, but turned the other way in bed, and said his prayers, he said to her, {...} works of the Devil, it was better to trust in God, and the same could and would help him in time. So she said, he should get up to drink with her, which he also did not want to do. Thereupon she left in the morning, and as soon as she left his house, his child, a boy at that time about 5 years old, cried the whole time, he carried on like that for two days. He said to the fellow in his house, Stoffel Jürgens, "Nobody did this to my child except your drinking-sister, therefore get out, and tell the same to take this away from the child again, or I will have

---

1 Of September. For names of the months, see p. xlii.
2 From the record.
3 The root of the mandrake is sometimes shaped like a person, and was believed to have magical properties in addition to its medicinal properties. They were sometimes kept on the mantle for good luck. We do not know the origin of the belief that a mandrake could move of its own accord: it is not impossible that Tempel Anneke herself invented the idea.

her be dealt with another way." The same went to her in Harxbüttel, and threatened to hit her until she was crooked and lame. After that his child got well again /: *as the notorious woman said to the fellow, "Go back, there is nothing wrong with the boy"*:/,[1] with which he certifies his testimony *in silentium*.[2]

---

1 The symbol /: ... :/ is used by the court scribe to indicate his own comments inserted into the text. See p. xlii.
2 Solemnly

Document C

[This document records legal action against Hans Tiehmann for hiring Tempel Anneke to perform sorcery. This incident was the origin of the criminal charges against Tempel Anneke. It was originally filed without a cover at the back of the collection.]

Extract Protocolli in the fines office
The 9th *Aprilis*[1] *Anno* 1663
Concerning Hans Tiehmann

Received 16th *Junii Anno 1663*

Actum in Brunswick in the fines office, the 9th *Aprilis Anno* 1663

Hans Tiehmann, the roofer, is summoned and questioned, whether recently something was stolen from him, and because of that, since he wanted to get his lost things back, he sought advice from Tempel Anneke of Harxbüttel, as she was supposed to be a notorious witch. Thereupon he gave as answer that not long ago some tinware and sausages were stolen from his house, and as he wanted very much to know where the stolen goods went to, he was directed to Tempel Anneke by the *Veltesche*.[2] How he then came to the same, complained to the same about his concerns, and as she revealed to him that his things would not be very far away, gave her 9*mg* as payment.

Hereupon it is decreed through civic regulations, that Tiehmann is fined 6*mr*. However, the *Veltesche*, because she gave instruction, is fined 3*mr* for that, which fine should be applied in accordance with the scope of the ordinance of the local Civic Regulations.[3]

J. Pilgram[4]

---

1   Of April. For names of the months, see p. xlii.
2   Anna Graven, wife of Cordt Velte.
3   These regulations are translated on p. 152.
4   The court scribe. For more discussion on the role of the officers, see pp. xxxv–xxxvii.

Folio 1

[The original of this document is now lost. It records the testimony of the five witnesses who were first called to give evidence against Tempel Anneke following her arrest. For the sources of this document, see pp. xxxiv-xxxv of the Introduction.]

Five persons appeared on the 25th of June, 1663, at the Neustadt Municipal Hall[1] in Brunswick, who testified in front of the judge to the following:

The first witness, Hans Tiehmann, citizen and roofer in Brunswick-Neustadt, testified that at the end of the year 1662, during the night, seven tin bowls, a tin mug, a tin bottle, tin spoons, various foodstuffs, grain, etc., were stolen from him. Because he wanted to know where his stolen goods were, a woman he knew advised him to go to the village of Harxbüttel. There a knowledgeable woman was supposed to live, the widow of Hans Kage, usually called Tempel Anneke. He should let her read his hand. She is supposed to know everything. When he arrived in Harxbüttel Tempel Anneke said to him that he may simply return home again. She would frighten the thief so much that he would get his belongings back in 24 hours. He should return in three days. Then he gave her an Ortstaler as a tip and went home again. The next morning, to his surprise, the tin bowls and the tin bottle were lying in front of his neighbour's door. When he returned to Harxbüttel three days later, Tempel Anneke told him that the thief was a poor man with two children; she had pegged the fellow into a hole so that the same had squeaked inside it like a heap of mice. Of the remaining stolen goods he didn't see anything else other than a tin mug.

The second witness was the publican of the Tempel pub in Harxbüttel, Hans Harves. He explained: about five weeks ago Tempel Anneke had several *Stübchen*[2] of beer fetched from him. In the evening of the same day she wanted another *Stübchen* of beer. But he gave her no more, but sent word that she had already drunk enough during the day. The following night he suddenly woke up because of a pain in his leg. When he looked for the cause he saw that a blister as big as a plate had developed on his ankle bone. Because

---

1 The preliminary investigation occurs in Neustadt, possibly because Tiehmann lived there. Once the criminal investigation commenced the trial was moved to the Higher Court in Hagen.

2 A *Stübchen* was a jug of about 3½ litres. In 1660 a *Stübchen* of beer cost 10 groschen.

of that he sent word to Tempel Anneke and told her that he had the injury on his leg from her, because she wanted to revenge herself that he had given her no more beer. She should come to answer for herself or remove the injury. Everyone in the village takes Tempel Anneke for a witch and a sorceress. She knows how to bring back lost things and cures animals with magical potions.

Anna Steinmann, the wife of the aforesaid Hans Harves, had the following to report: before Shrove Tuesday she had a swollen hand. Tempel Anneke gave her a remedy against it, which sometimes helped more and sometimes helped less. At any rate, as everyone can see, the hand has not improved yet. Also on one occasion Tempel Anneke had the already half decomposed head of an animal brought to her house. Afterwards she threw the head into the water. When her husband crossed the river in his boat a few days later, he probably got the injury to his leg from the rotting head. Also she knew that Tempel Anneke had not visited the church for twenty years, and also had not been to the table of the Lord in this same time.

The following witness, Hennig Roleffes, a resident of Wenden, explained that in the previous year a bad plague broke out amongst the sheep in Harxbüttel, so that many died. Tempel Anneke was asked to help. She then baked a sheep to powder in the oven and administered that to the sheep, whereupon all became healthy again. The following day he suddenly took ill. In great pain he had to lie in his bed and acquired holes in his leg as long as fingers. Neither Tempel Anneke nor another healing woman could cure him, even though he gave the first three Taler and a goose. Finally he went to the trouser tailor, Jochen, in Brunswick. This one cured him so that he can now stand and walk again.

The fifth and last witness was Autor Bahrensdorff from Watenbüttel near Brunswick. He testified: six years ago two horses as well as a foal disappeared from the field during the night. When he came another day to the house of the wheelmaker, Thies, and complained to him of his bad fortune, by coincidence Tempel Anneke was present as well, and called out when she heard his story about the theft: "Autor, you are a fool. Your horses are walking there in front of the woods." When he left the town and came to the open field, look—there his horses were standing by the Ölper marsh in front of the woods at the city wall.

Folio 2

[This folio contains a list of questions about which Tempel Anneke was interrogated on July 1, 1663. (See Folio 3.) The questions were drafted by the
Syndicus of the Higher Court based on reports of Tempel Anneke's activities
collected in the period prior to the trial. In accordance with legal practice
at the time, the questions were prepared before they were put to Tempel
Anneke. For a full description of the original layout of questions and answers
in the archival source, see pp. xxxiv-xxxv.]

1. What the name of the questioned is and where she was born,

2. How old she is and how she supports herself,

3. Whether she was put in school in her youth,

4. Whether she learned the Ten Commandments,

5. Whether she knew the other commandment,

6. Whether she understands what is forbidden in it,

7. How long it was since she had been to the table of the Lord or the Holy
   Communion,

8. Whether she knows Hans Tiehmann,

9. Whether he didn't ask her for advice concerning several stolen articles,

10. Whether she didn't promise him that she would be able to frighten
    the thief who stole what belonged to him, so that before 24 hours had
    passed, he should have his things back,

11. Whether she asked him to come back to her on the 3rd day after,

12. Whether she didn't get an Ortstaler[1] from Tiehmann as a tip,

---

1   For background on currency, see p. xxxviii–xxxix.

13. Whether she didn't frighten the thief, as she had promised, so that he brought back some of the stolen things of Tiehmann's,

14. How and in which way did she do it,

15. Whether she didn't plug the thief into a drilled hole in the name of the Evil Enemy, so that the fellow squeaked inside it like a heap of mice,

16. How did she know how the fellow, who stole from Tiehmann, fed himself, and how many children he had,

17. Whether she hadn't been asked on one occasion to come to the toll collector Bahrensdorff,

18. Whether she hadn't been with the same, or come to him, and what did she do while she was there,

19. Whether some weeks ago she didn't order several Stübchen of beer on credit from Hans Harves, otherwise Tempel Hans,

20. Whether she didn't that same day want to borrow more from him but didn't get it,

21. Whether, because he would not let her have any, she didn't conjure an injury into his thigh,

22. How she accomplished this,

23. Whether Hennig Vaddrian on the Knochenhauer Street in Hagen didn't once come to her because of an injury like that,

24. Whether Harves didn't let her be told through the same, that he got his ailment from no one else but her,

25. Whether she wasn't threatened, if she wouldn't remove the injury from him, that he would look for help in another place,

26. Whether he didn't add that, if she were innocent, she should come and answer the charge,

27. Why did she stay away, and also gave no answer to the butcher,[1]

28. Whether a soldier's wife here, called the *Henkelmannische*,[2] on Reichen Street, isn't known to her, and from where,

29. Whether the same had not been with *Inquisitin*[3] on her farm this winter, and what she had wanted there,

30. Whether she didn't bring the High Countess of Lehre to her,

31. What business the High Countess had with her,

32. Whether her advice wasn't needed because of 6 lost ducats,

33. What kind of advice she gave, and whether she got the ducats back,

34. Whether, years ago when the cows at Harxbüttel were dying, she didn't administer something to the cattle against that,

35. What it was, and how she prepared it,

36. Whether it helped the cattle, and the dying stopped from that,

37. From whom did she learn this, and whether this didn't happen through sorcery,

38. Whether she didn't conjure something into the left arm of the housewife of Hans Harves, that spread to the left hand and made the hand swell thickly,

39. Whether she didn't give this woman something, that was supposed to help again,

---

1   I.e., Hennig Vaddrian.
2   I.e., Dorothea Mehrdorff, wife of Hans Henkelmann.
3   "The accused or investigated," i.e., Tempel Anneke.

40. Yet, why this didn't help her,

41. Whether she didn't order Lüdecke Tau's wife to bring the head of a dead animal from Bortfeld into the house of *Inquisitin*,

42. What did she do with it, and what did she need it for,

43. Whether she didn't throw the head into the water so that when Hans Harves rowed over the spot, he should get the injury to the leg,

44. Whether she didn't offer to help them when dying befell the sheep in Harxbüttel,

45. Whether she didn't bring the dying amongst the sheep through sorcery,

46. How, and by which means, did she want to help the sheep,

47. Whether she didn't burn a sheep from the herd to powder in the oven, cooked something in a kettle, and administered it to the sheep,

48. Whether she didn't learn such things from the Evil Enemy,

49. Whether she didn't conjure something into the left leg of Hennig Roleffes of Wenden, so that it broke open,

50. Whether whenever he caught sight of her his whole body swelled thickly, and this happened four times,

51. For what reasons, and how did she do this,

52. Whether he didn't give her 3 Taler and a goose, so that she should help him again,

53. Whether at the wedding of the sheep master of Harxbüttel she didn't say to the wife of Hans Vette, that she could lock and unlock[1] and that Hennig Roleffes must still do better,

---

1   For the meaning of this term, see the Introduction, p. xl.

54. Why she didn't help him,

55. Whether she didn't conjure the evil things into the head of Jürgen Roleffes, so that he turned completely dense from it,

56. How she did it, and from where did she get the evil things,

57. Whether six years ago she didn't inform Autor Bahrensdorff where his horses and foals could be found, which he believed to be lost,

58. Where did she know it from,

59. Whether at that time she didn't want to help two sick children of Lüdecke Thies, the wheel maker here, and how did that go,

60. Whether she didn't use such forbidden arts more, where, on whom, how, and how long,

61. Whether she didn't make a pact with the Evil Enemy, and through his help committed such deeds,

62. How and in which form did he come to her, how did she join together with him,

63. Whether she didn't do harm to people, animals, or also to crops,

64. How was she able to do it each time, and didn't the Evil Spirit tell her to and teach her,

65. Whether she fornicated with the same in unnatural ways, how often and at which place,

66. Whether through this means she was able to bring about the evil things.

Folio 3

[This folio contains Tempel Anneke's answers to the questions drawn up in Folio 2. In the original records, Tempel Anneke's answers were always recorded in a separate folio without the questions. Here and elsewhere we have reprinted the questions to avoid the need to read back and forth between the folios.]

The answers of the imprisoned Anna Roleffes, otherwise called Tempel Anneke, given without torture, regarding the *Inquisitionalis*[1] formulated in *Act. num.* 2.[2]

The 1st of July 1663

Actum in the municipal jail of Hagen on the 1st of July *Anno* 1663.

By the honourable Gabriel Oeding, officer of the court, also Johann Velhagen and Otto Theune, both magistrates of the court, and Johann Pilgram, the court scribe.

The imprisoned Tempel Anneke was questioned without torture according to the *Inquisitional Articul*[3] formulated *Sub Num. Actor*,[4] there she gave her answers as follows on each *Formalibus verbis*[5]

1. *What the name of the questioned is and where she was born,*
   Says, her name is Anna Roleffes, her husband lived in Harxbüttel, was named Hans Kage, and she had been born in Harxbüttel.

2. *How old she is and how she supports herself,*
   Says, when Duke Heinrich besieged this town, when it rained so much, she was five years old. She supported herself with her husband, as long as he was alive, through working in the fields on the farm in Harxbüttel,

---

1   "Questions." Usually *Inquisition* means "investigation," but sometimes, as here, it means "question."
2   "In proceeding number 2"; i.e., Folio 2.
3   "Investigation question."
4   "Under the proceedings."
5   "Using the proper words."

where her son, Hans Kage, now still lives. Because her mother, Ilse Lilie, in her youth served for five years as a maid with a barber[1] near Wolfsburg, at which place she couldn't name, and saw there and learned how he healed people and made them something, which she also made use of later, in that she helped people with balms and the like for the body and the holy thing, *Inquisitin* had watched her mother, how she did it. And she helped people in this way, not only while her husband was alive, but after he died, when he was stabbed through outside Wolfenbüttel / : *Anno 1641, the 3rd 7bris :/* [2] in her widowed station, whatever the people had wrong with them, in the stone, liver and lung, when people drank too quickly. How she read and learned such from her herbal books of which she had two.

3. *Whether she was put in school in her youth,*
Says, yes.

4. *Whether she learned the Ten Commandments,*
Says, yes, went for three years to Mr. Fredrich, to the church, because he taught children there, after he had been let go in Sampleben.

5. *Whether she knew the other commandment,*
Says, yes.

6. *Whether she understands what is forbidden in it,*
Says, yes, one should not do sorcery, not lie and cheat.

7. *How long it was since she had been to the table of the Lord or the Holy Communion,*
Says, two years ago, here in Brunswick, then she was at the Altstadt Market with the old *Christsche,*[3] because Herr Jürgen in Gross Schwülper didn't want to take her until she brought him a letter from Gardelegen. When the soldiers pulled out of Wolfenbüttel, and she had no more means of support, she went to a mayor in Gardelegen, Friedrich Hillenbrandt, and served the same for five years.

---

1   In the early modern period, barbers also provided basic medical care.

2   We do not know the circumstances of her husband's death.

3   This is a woman's name.

8. *Whether she knows Hans Tiehmann,*
Says, yes, she had seen him before, she wanted to rightly confirm that.

9. *Whether he didn't ask her for advice concerning several stolen articles,*
Says, yes.

10. *Whether she didn't promise him that she would be able to frighten the thief who stole what belonged to him, so that before 24 hours had passed, he should have his things back,*
Says she didn't do that, how would she come to do such a thing. What she had seen, there she could give information, but nothing else.

11. *Whether she asked him to come back to her on the 3rd day after,*
Says, no, she didn't send for him again. Instead around Holy Three Kings Day[1] Tiehmann was at her place in Harxbüttel, and asked her for advice, whether she couldn't divine his stolen things for him. To that she answered him, that she couldn't divine. Rather such things as he missed, namely a bottle and a tin bowl, a woman had for sale in a basket in a small stall at the market in Altewieck, that *Inquisitin* had seen it there.

12. *Whether she didn't get an Ortstaler from Tiehmann as a tip,*
Says, yes, for having told him where his things were.

13. *Whether she didn't frighten the thief, as she had promised, so that he brought back some of the stolen things of Tiehmann's,*
Says no, how would she come to do that, how would that happen.

14. *How and in which way did she do it,*
Cessat.[2]

15. *Whether she didn't plug the thief into a drilled hole in the name of the Evil Enemy, so that the fellow squeaked inside it like a heap of mice?*
Says, that isn't true in eternity.

---

1   This is Epiphany, January 6.
2   "Remains silent." This indicates that Tempel Anneke does not answer the question.

16. *How did she know how the fellow, who stole from Tiehmann, fed himself, and how many children he had,*

    Says, she didn't say that, also didn't know it and still didn't know it, there could be any rascal accusing of her of things she hadn't done, they couldn't say that.

17. *Whether she hadn't been asked on one occasion to come to the toll collector Bahrensdorff,*

    Says, yes, and she spent two nights in the house with the *Bahrensdorffische.*[1]

18. *Whether she hadn't been with the same, or come to him, and what did she do while she was there,*

    Says, the *Bahrensdorffische* had /: *respectfully reported* :/an illness of the womb, the accused prescribed herbs for her, those were brought by the maids from the apothecary and cooked with wine, she also received money.

19. *Whether some weeks ago she didn't order several Stübchen of beer on credit from Hans Harves, otherwise Tempel Hans,*

    Says, yes.

20. *Whether she didn't that same day want to borrow more from him but didn't get it,*

    Says, yes, and that he often sent the empty jug back to her.

21. *Whether, because he would not let her have any, she didn't conjure an injury into his thigh,*

    Says no, there our Lord God would save her, they had been good friends all the days of their lives.

22. *How she accomplished this,*

    Cessat.

23. *Whether Hennig Vaddrian on the Knochenhauer Street in Hagen didn't once come to her because of an injury like that,*

    Says she knows nothing about it, the publican got it into his leg for the very first time 14 days ago, how could he have sent Vaddrian to her.

---

1   The wife of Bahrensdorff.

24. *Whether Harves didn't let her be told through the same, that he got his ailment from no one else but her,*
Says, no.

25. *Whether she wasn't threatened, if she wouldn't remove the injury from him, that he would look for help in another place,*
Says, neither Vaddrian nor the publican had said anything to her, had either of them asked *Inquisitin*, she would have wanted to give the same an answer.

26. *Whether he didn't add that, if she were innocent, she should come and answer the charge,*
Says, no.

27. *Why did she stay away, and also gave no answer to the butcher,*
Cessat.

28. *Whether a soldier's wife here, called the Henkelmannische, on Reichen Street, isn't known to her, and from where,*
Says, yes, has long known her well.

29. *Whether the same had not been with Inquisitin on her farm this winter, and what she had wanted there,*
Says, once, three or four times, and had with her a woman from Lehre.

30. *Whether she didn't bring the High Countess of Lehre to her,*
Says, yes, she had been told that it was the High Countess.

31. *What business the High Countess had with her,*
Says, the High Countess said that she had lost 6 ducats, and asked *Inquisitin* if she couldn't give her news, but *Inquisitin* answered she didn't know anything about it.

32. *Whether her advice wasn't needed because of 6 lost ducats,*
Says as *ad proxe praecedentem Inquisitionalem.*[1]

---

1 "With respect to the preceding investigation." However, here and in some other places the intended meaning is more likely "preceding question."

33. *What kind of advice she had given, and whether she got the ducats back,*
Says, she said she should look for the ducats, whether they were maybe misplaced, and *Inquisitin* had heard that the ducats were found again under the documents of the High Count in his pants pocket. And the High Countess gave her an Ortstaler as a tip since she said that it should be looked for.

34. *Whether, years ago when the cows at Harxbüttel were dying, she didn't administer something to the cattle against that,*
Says, yes.

35. *What it was, and how she prepared it,*
Says it was herbs,[1] that she herself bought from the big apothecary, namely chicory roots, Christmas rose, field hops, lungwort, watercress, wild sage, to add to that she scraped the berries off the top of buckthorn and cooked it together with water. To this she took a hind quarter of a dead 1 year old calf after it was cut up, and after she baked the same in the oven to a powder, she mixed it with the aforesaid herbs and what cooked out of it, and administered it to the healthy cattle, three times a day in the name of our Lord Jesus Christ, in the name of God, not in the name of the Evil One. Also some people gave it themselves to their cattle in the name of God and asked *Inquisitin* that she should make something for their cattle. The reported hind quarter she also put in the oven in the name of God, and from each farmer she got half a *Stübchen* of beer for it.

36. *Whether it helped the cattle, and the dying stopped from that,*
Says, yes.

37. *From whom did she learn this, and whether this didn't happen through sorcery,*
Says, from the cow herds, they also cooked something for the cattle, they had also said, when there is a lot of dying among the cattle, that from those dead cattle some should be fried to powder and the dying of cattle would diminish, if this is sorcery or worked through sorcery she wouldn't know, had never understood that, if it were so, wouldn't want

---

1   Appendix B contains a list of the herbs mentioned in the records. See also Figure 8 on p. 162, an engraving of Christmas Rose.

to do it again in her living days, who would want to have some, should make their own.

38. *Whether she didn't conjure something into the left arm of the housewife of Hans Harves, that spread to the left hand and made the hand swell thickly,*
Says no, that would have to be proven, God should save her from that, to think that she would come to teach such and such evil deeds what she did with her medicine, that was something different.

39. *Whether she didn't give this woman something, that was supposed to help again,*
Says, yes, she smoked the same with juniper berries and told her that she should hold this onto it in the name of God.

40. *Yet, why this didn't help her,*
Says, if God didn't want to allow that it would help, what could she do about it, much is used that doesn't help.

41. *Whether she didn't order Lüdecke Tau's wife to bring the head of a dead animal from Bortfeld into the house of Inquisitin,*
Says no, she didn't order that, but said to the same, that she should fry the head to powder in Bortfeld, and to administer it to the animals, but when Lüdecke Tau's wife brought the head, *Inquisitin* threw the same into the water in Harxbüttel.

42. *What did she do with it, and what did she need it for,*
Says *ad proxe praecedentem Inquisitionalem.*

43. *Whether she didn't throw the head into the water so that when Hans Harves rowed over the spot, he should get the injury to the leg,*
Says, yes, she threw it into the water, but that it happened in order to give Harves a lame leg and an injury in it, that wasn't so.

44. *Whether she didn't offer to help them when dying befell the sheep in Harxbüttel,*
Says no, but when she was talked to about it, she said she could not help the sheep, as she also couldn't help the sheep, because several things had befallen the sheep, that they died from consumption and they choked on their blood.

45. *Whether she didn't bring the dying amongst the sheep through sorcery,*
Says no, God should save her, whether nothing in the world could die except through sorcery, as if God couldn't send it to people.

46. *How, and by which means, did she want to help the sheep,*
Says, she didn't help the sheep, and also could not do it.

47. *Whether she didn't burn a sheep from the herd to powder in the oven, cooked something in a kettle, and administered it to the sheep,*
Says that the *Schaffmeisterse*[1] did that herself, she is still alive and *Inquisitin* had not agreed with her about this.

48. *Whether she didn't learn such things from the Evil Enemy,*
Cessat.

49. *Whether she didn't conjure something into the left leg of Hennig Roleffes of Wenden, so that it broke open,*
Says no: instead Hennig Roleffes had a disease /: *salva venia*[2] :/ on top of his genitals and had four or five small holes in it, she healed him and 3 holes she had closed with resin, wax and boar lard, the remaining holes the said Hennig Roleffes had healed in Brunswick, *Inquisitin* didn't know by whom, and at that time she got a half Taler.

50. *Whether whenever he caught sight of her his whole body swelled thickly, and this happened four times,*
Says, that isn't so, Roleffes could not say that.

51. *For what reasons, and how did she do this,*
Cessat.

52. *Whether he didn't give her 3 Taler and a goose, so that she should help him again,*
Says, he didn't give her that, had only received a half Taler, even though he had promised her 3 Taler without a goose, because his mother was supposed give out the goose, how does the rogue dare to lie like that.

---

1   The wife of the sheep master.

2   "I beg your pardon." It was a common practice for court scribes to insert such comments when "impolite" or blasphemous testimony is given.

53. *Whether at the wedding of the sheep master of Harxbüttel she didn't say to the wife of Hans Vette, that she could lock and unlock and that Henning Roleffes must still do better,*
Cessat.

54. *Why she didn't help him,*
Says that she wasn't able to help the same, because the disease was too big.

55. *Whether she didn't conjure the evil things into the head of Jürgen Roleffes, so that he turned completely dense from it,*
Says, "The almighty God save us from that, for that I have prayed many a Lord's Prayer, dear Jesus Christ, who would want to do anything to him."

56. *How she did it, and from where did she get the evil things,*
Cessat.

57. *Whether six years ago she didn't inform Autor Bahrensdorff where his horses and foals could be found, which he had believed to be lost,*
Says no, he could not say that.

58. *Where had she known it from,*
Cessat.

59. *Whether at that time she didn't want to help two sick children of Lüdecke Thies, the wheel maker here, and how did that go,*
Says, even though she was in the house, she had not been able to help the children, because their spleen had a growth on it.

60. *Whether she didn't use such forbidden arts more, where, on whom, how, and how long,*
Says she didn't know any arts, she could do what she told them about, for that she had her books, and she knew of no people, who came to her, and she couldn't treat them, when they needed something against a "quick drink." That all happened through God's help and remedies.

61. *Whether she didn't make a pact with the Evil Enemy, and through his help committed such deeds,*
Says, no, she didn't make a pact, her dear Jesus Christ should save her from this, she had nothing to do with the Evil Spirit.

62. *How and in which form did he come to her, how did she join together with him,*
Cessat.

63. *Whether she didn't do harm to people, animals or also to crops,*
Says, no.

64. *How was she able to do it each time, and didn't the Evil Spirit tell her to and teach her,*
Says, she has no business with the Evil Spirit.

65. *Whether she fornicated with the same in unnatural ways, how often and at which place,*
Says no, spit right away on the ground, saying "Pfui, I should have anything to do with the Dirt, go away with that, how should I commit myself to sin in this way?"

66. *Whether through this means she was able to bring about the evil things,*
Cessat.

Folio 4

[This document indicates the commencement of the trial proper. In accordance with the Carolina, the initial evidence recorded in Folio 1 to 3 is here determined to be sufficient to proceed to a full criminal investigation. For the background on the Carolina, see pp. xxx-xxxiii of the Introduction.]

Decretum[1] the 3rd of July 1663
Concerning the imprisoned Anna Roleffes

Inquisition Acte[2] against the imprisoned Anna Roleffes, the officials and magistrates of the court are ordered to have the witnesses who testified summarily confirm their testimony concerning *Inquisitional* articles with an oath. And when they have done that to confront them with the *Inquisitin*, also to write down and to register all and each one of the testimonies carefully, in order that what will happen is what is just.

Proclaimed before the General Council
The 3rd of July 1663

J. Strauch[3]

---

1   "Decree."
2   "Investigation proceedings."
3   Johann Strauch, *Syndicus*.

Folio 5

[In accordance with the instructions given in Folio 4, the witnesses who gave evidence in Folio 1 are here required to give their testimony under oath. The third witness, Anna Steinmann, failed to appear. The fourth witness in Folio 1, Hennig Roleffes, lived in Wenden, outside Brunswick, and so his sworn testimony is requested from the officials in Neubrück, which was the administrative centre of that district. That letter is recorded in Folio 10, and his sworn testimony is in Folio 18.]

The confirmation by oath of Hans Tiehmann, Hans Harves, and Autor Bahrensdorff

The 8th of July *Anno* 1663

Actum in the municipal hall of Hagen

The 8th of July *Anno* 1663

By the honourable Gabriel Oeding, officer of the court, also Johann Velhagen and Otto Theune both magistrates of the court, and Johann Pilgram the court scribe.

Following the *Decreto* of July 3rd declared before the *E.E.*[1] General Council, the persons mentioned below are interrogated once more about their summary testimony:

1. *Testis*[2]
Hans Tiehmann, when he was clearly and carefully again presented with his given summary testimony from the 25th of June in *Actis. Num. 1.*,[3] did not only stand consistently by it after many serious admonitions and warnings, but added this, when he came to Tempel Anneke in the way already told, that the same had then told him he would not get the *Fresselwaren* /: *food* :/

---

1   *Ein Ehrenveste* "knightly"
2   "Witness." Hans Tiehmann is "Witness 1," etc.
3   "In proceeding number 1."

back, *Item*[1] that she ordered him, when he would come back to town, to boast righteously and to say in the street so that the people will hear it, that he would burn /: *salva venia* :/ the thief's ass, or have it set on fire. But he had not wanted to say such things. In this way the witness was then able to confirm this, his testimony, *gravia admonitione de evitando perjurio ejusq. atrocissima poena*,[2] with an oath made in person.

2. *Testis*

Hans Harves was presented with his summary testimony clearly and distinctly together with the added secondary question of the 25th of June in *Act. Num.* 1., and he not only stood firmly and consistently by it, but also confirmed this his testimony, and to what was appended to the testimony, with an oath made in person, and specifically following previous careful warnings against perjury and the severe penalty for it.

3. *Testis*

Anna Steinmann, the housewife of Hans Harves, was also supposed to confirm her testimony, and was summoned because of that, only her husband indicated that she had a bad seizure, because of which her head swelled so badly, that she could barely speak, even less come in front of people. Because of that, the confirmation by oath, and the confrontation regarding this person to be done after the findings, must be omitted for now.

4. *Testis*

Autor Bahrensdorff was presented again with his testimony from *Num Actor.* 1, given the 25th of June, and he stood consistently by it, he also confirmed the same with an oath made in person, *gravia admonitione de evitando perjurio ejusq. atrocissima poena.*

---

1   "Also," "likewise."

2   "With a strong warning about avoiding perjury and its severe penalty."

Folio 6

[The instructions in Folio 4 require that after their testimony is given under oath each witness who testified in Folio 1 is to be confronted with Tempel Anneke about the differences between their testimony and hers. This folio records the confrontations of Tempel Anneke with Hans Tiehmann and Autor Bahrensdorff.]

Confrontatio[1]
Hans Tiehmann with the imprisoned
The 8th of July *Anno* 1663

Confrontatio
Autor Bahrensdorff with the imprisoned
The 9th of July *Anno* 1663

Act. eod. Die a meridie[2]

Confrontatio

Further following the *Decreto* mentioned at the outset, the imprisoned Tempel Anneke, previously interrogated without torture about the *Articulos Inquisitionalis*[3] contained in *sub Num. Actor* 2—which she denied the 1st of July in *Actis Num.* 3, namely about questions 10, 11, 12, 13, 15, 16 and 21—is questioned again without torture. And considering the pressing nature of the affair after the findings, Hans Tiehmann was confronted with the same about each question individually, after she had just testified:

10. *Whether she didn't promise him that she would be able to frighten the thief who stole what belonged to him, so that before 24 hours had passed, he should have his things back,*
    Says, she didn't do this, that was not true.

---

1 "Confrontation [with witnesses]."
2 "Proceeding on the same day at noon."
3 "Investigation questions."

Upon this, Hans Tiehmann was confronted with the imprisoned, and said to the same consistently to her face, she had distinctly told him that, in that way had agreed and promised. And the witness added, that what he testified and swore to this morning, and that was put forward to him now again from the article, really was true, as God should help him in body and soul, then he immediately struck his chest, and said, that he isn't a child nor a boy, but knew very well what he spoke.

The imprisoned stood steadfastly by her denial. But when she was seriously spoken to and it was put to her that she should take it seriously to heart, that she should keep in mind, that there is a God in heaven who sees and knows everything, that she herself just now had heard that which the witness had told her to her face, she said, yes, yes, yes, she had said that, but was sorry, did not want to do it again, wanted to swear an oath to an honourable council, that in the future she will not tell something to anybody or give news, until eternity even if her own bodily son were to come.

11. *Whether she asked him to come back to her on the 3rd day after,*
    Says, yes, she had certainly thought about it carefully five times.[1]

Cessat Confrontatio.[2]

13. *Whether she didn't frighten the thief, as she had promised, so that he brought back some of the stolen things of Tiehmann's,*
    Says, yes, she had taken a small linen *Blümerken* /: *a little piece* :/ from the shirt of an old man, and had wrapped the same around a stick, a plug, that she had just found in her yard. And on her son's farm in the stable, the pig stable on the right towards the door when you walk in, hit the linen together with the stick, which was a plug, into a drilled hole in square /: *rough* :/ wood, with a rock that she could hold in her hand in the name of God, not in the name of the Evil One. And after three days, after she hit the plug loose again, pulled it out again, and tossed or threw the aforementioned piece from an old shirt into the yard, then it was a small piece of a linen child's cloth, which before was the shirt of a man so that one could recognize the sleeve or waistband.

---

1   Tempel Anneke's response here is probably in anger at the urging to think carefully about her answers.
2   "End of the confrontation."

15. *Whether she didn't plug the thief into a drilled hole in the name of the Evil Enemy, so that the fellow squeaked inside it like a heap of mice,*

Says, she didn't do more than hit it once, and said, "There you stick in the name of God," and it was true that she said, the fellow should squeak like mice. Why don't such fellows give up their stealing.

16. *How did she know how the fellow, who stole from Tiehmann, fed himself, and how many children he had,*

Says, no.[1]

Now when Tiehmann was confronted with the imprisoned and told her his previous testimony to her face, how he succinctly testified and swore to today, that she, *Captiva*,[2] had talked to him at that time. At first she declared, that she had talked in that way, and she had forgotten. But when she was urged to tell the truth, she admitted that she had talked in that way, and that because of her knowledge she answered in the beginning, that she had seen how the linen or the linen *Blümeken* had moved. Thereupon one wanted to know more accurately from her, and asked once more about the sources of her knowledge. She gave as her reply, how, as mentioned before, she knocked the plug out of the drilled hole again together with the linen *Blümen*, and when she was alone in her son's house threw both together into the fire on the hearth, so that she saw three shining or bright sparks fly up from the fire into the air. From this she learned that it was a man, the same had two children, but the plug burned away together with the linen.

Questioned whether she knew that Tiehmann would not get back the lost food of lard, sausage, flour and cheese, which she called in a single word, edible goods.

Says, if the thief had not been hungry, he would not have stolen, one can think that easily.

Further questioned, whether she didn't say to Tiehmann, when he was back in town, that he should righteously boast, and say in the street so that the people can hear, that he would burn the thief's ass, or have it set on fire, and why she ordered Tiehmann to do this.

Says finally yes, because in this way the thief would be frightened so that he would return the stolen things.

---

1   The answer here does not match the written form of question 16. Perhaps they asked, "Did she know …?"

2   Prisoner in custody, i.e., Tempel Anneke.

Further asked, why she said to Tiehmann, if he hadn't come on that day, that his things would have been bundled together and sold in Wolfenbüttel, and how she knew this.

Says, said it in order that Tiehmann would get his things back, and she knew all of that because she had hammered the piece of wood in, and since it was put into the drilled hole the fellow couldn't take the things any further away.

Actum the 9th of July *Anno* 1663

The imprisoned was further questioned again about the 57th and 58th *Inquisitionalem*, and Autor Bahrensdorff was confronted with her regarding this. Then the imprisoned testified:

Ad.[1]
57. *Whether six years ago she didn't inform Autor Bahrensdorff where his horses and foals could be found, which he had believed to be lost,*
Says again, no.

Hereupon Bahrensdorff is presented to her, and said to her face that she had spoken such words to him at that time, as described in his summary testimony. But she gave as answer to that that she didn't know that any more, even if she had said that, which she really doesn't know, whether that were a sin. She might have waved with her hand, but that doesn't mean she was able to divine.

Now as the witness stood consistently by his testimony, that it had been like that, the imprisoned said that she is now remembering that it was true, she had said that in fact the horses had not been stolen, and so for them there was no divining necessary, had only lifted her hand and said, "There they go in front of the woods."

58. *Where did she know it from,*
Says, she only said that, she didn't know it from anywhere.

Asked whether one time she didn't get half a Taler and a further 6g.[2] from

---

1   "With respect to"
2   I.e., 6 *groschen*. For a discussion of local currency in early modern times, see pp. xxxviii-xxxix.

Autor Bahrensdorff, and why did this happen?

Says, yes, she received the money, and brought it to Cordt Tellig, a former cowherd here in Hagen, because the cattle of the brother of the imprisoned in Harxbüttel were partially sick and partially dead. With that the aforesaid cowherd was supposed to help. Now as the cowherd got the half Taler and 6g. worth of fish, he had said to the imprisoned that she should tell the people that they should give the cattle rue and their own manure mixed with vinegar, that way the cattle should not die anymore, which the imprisoned passed on again to her brother.

Folio 7

[This folio records the testimony of witnesses who lived on Kaiser Street, where Hans Tiehmann lived, concerning Tempel Anneke's activities there and the theft of Thiehmann's goods. Also in this folio, Dorothea Mehrdorff, the wife of Hans Henkelmann, is questioned and confronted with Tempel Anneke concerning the latter's answers to questions 28 to 33 in Folio 3.]

The testimony of Cordt Velte, his housewife and both the housewives of Hans Dietgen and Hans Henkelmann

The 9th of July *Anno* 1663

Actum in the Municipal Jail in Hagen

The 9th of July *Anno* 1663

By the appointed persons of the court of the municipality of Hagen.

1 . *Testis*
Cordt Velte, *admonitus de veritate dicenda*[1] reports that he knows nothing about the imprisoned and her business, he does not keep company with her, nor could he give news of how she carried on, he also didn't know who stole the belongings of the roofer, and even less who had put the tin ware in the morning in front of the witness' front door. The *Mollerse*, otherwise called the *Thiesche*, would know the best information.

2 . *Testis*
Anna Graven, Cordt Velte's housewife, *admonita de veritate dicenda*, reports that, during the plague they had had a sick fuller,[2] right across from her husband's house on Kaiser Street, who was afflicted, as was said, /: *respectfully reported* :/ on the genitals, and he had such pain in that place that often he screamed day and night, and he could not stand the terrible pain. Because of that he had to be kept under constant watch, so that he didn't harm

---

1 "He was warned that he must tell the truth."
2 A fuller is a person who cleans and softens raw fabric by treading on it in large vats.

himself. Tempel Anneke tended to this fuller with others, when he was lodging upstairs at Jochim Honnmeister's house, in that she brought herbs from the apothecary and made a bath in the tub for the poor person, the fuller. Through that the witness made the acquaintance of the said Tempel Anneke, so that at times when she came into town Tempel Anneke spoke with them in their house. But the witness has seen or heard nothing bad about her. And she remembers that at the time when things were well with the fuller, the men who were present teased Tempel Anneke, that she should read their palm, but the witness didn't know if this took place or did not take place.

Otherwise she remembers that she once had a farmer from Lyr in the house, the imprisoned looked in his hand, and wrote with chalk on the table, several strokes, and said "Hennig, you have stolen so many geese." And that had all been teasing, she didn't know any more about the stolen goods than what her husband will already have reported.

3. *Testis*
Agnesa Graten, Hans Dietgen's housewife, *admonita de veritate dicenda*, reports that Hans Tiehmann the roofer lived right across from them. Shortly before Epiphany goods were stolen from him, and for 14 days it was talked about, before the facts became known. At the same time they had a man called Martin Richter in their house as a tenant, and it so happened that she had lost a distaff. As she searched now and again for that reason, and finally she got to Martin Richter's small food cupboard, and looked behind the same, she noticed that a small linen cloth was lying behind it. But when she pulled the same out she became aware that behind the cupboard a large loaf of bread was lying there, from which a small piece had been cut off, and a bit further along a glowing or bright tin bowel, which didn't shock her a little, because she conjectured that it must be part of Thiemann's tin goods. Because of that she first told the *Mühische*,[1] then Herr Hermann Scharkopff, her father confessor, and told Herr Br. Jürgen Düvel,[2] who then ordered her to keep the bowl for safe-keeping until after the new Council took office, when she brought it to the house of Herr Br. Hermann Boess, and handed it over,

Asked, whether she didn't reveal this to the aforementioned Richter and his wife, how the same acted after that and how they felt.

---

1 A woman's name.
2 *Br.* stands for *Bürgermeister*, mayor. Düvel and Boess were the outgoing and incoming mayors of the municipality of Neustadt.

Says, she revealed to Martin Richter that she had found the bowl right there, and she had not taken him for that kind of a fellow. But he didn't answer her more than that he said and asked: "Who says?" Also in the meantime he looked really horrible and didn't speak another word, so that the witness was afraid of him. Richter's wife on the other hand wanted to admit nothing, but stated that she would sue anyone who would say this about them or about her husband.

Asked whether Martin Richter, after the theft had been committed, didn't go back and forth, and up and down the stairs, and was unable to rest, as if he had lost his mind?

Says no, he had been able to sleep, except that she heard, when she came to bed in the evening, and Richter's wife had not gone up yet, that Richter was lying in his room and said, "Oh! Oh! Poor me, poor me!" And that happened 14 days past the last Michaelmas[1] and about four evenings one after the other. Then the witness told this to Richter's wife, and asked her about it. She must have told it back to him, after that time the witness did not hear it any more.

4. *Testis*

Dorothea Mehrdorff, housewife of local soldier Hans Henkelmann, *admonita de veritate dicenda*, reports that, at the time the Constable was stabbed to death in the church square of St. Catharine's, Tempel Anneke could not leave by the city gate in the evening, and because of that she came to the door of the witness and asked for lodging, when she still lived at the big manorhouse of Herr Br. Düvel. And because another soldier's wife had given this Tempel Anneke a good recommendation, and had said where the same was from, the said Tempel Anneke was taken in by them and stayed two nights as a lodger. That is how the witness first came to know Tempel Anneke.

Four years ago her husband got it in his right hand, and the cowherd had told him to boil *heerössel*[2] and chervil with clear water, and to bandage his hand with it. And when Tempel Anneke heard about this, she said that the herbs were very good for that, and that the witness should go ahead and bathe her husband's hand with it.

Asked, how often was she at the imprisoned Tempel Anneke's,

---

1   The feast of St. Michael is September 29, so this statement does not fit with the date that the goods were stolen shortly before Epiphany, January 6.

2   The page is creased at this point, so this transcription is based on guesswork; we can assume, however, that it is some kind of herb.

Says, before this she had ordered flax from Tempel Anneke's son, had wanted to order this past Easter with the same again, had also been sent by her host[1] to Harxbüttel, so she was many times in Harxbüttel, but had not been specifically with Tempel Anneke. Except the one time, when she was healthy again after a broken leg, she went for the first time, with the *Beckerse*[2] on the hill and with the High Countess of Lehre, to Harxbüttel to Tempel Anneke, because the *Beckerse* had come to the house of the witness, so that she had to come out with them. And she was in the living room and had nothing to do with the affair. And the *Beckerse* and Tempel Anneke went with the High Countess in Harxbüttel by themselves out of the living room, so that the witness did not hear what they said or did.

Hereupon, the imprisoned Tempel Anneke was presented with her given testimony on the 1st of July in *Actis Num.* 3, and she was asked at the same time, how she could have answered in that way, since it wasn't like that. Then she answered, that because of her flax Henkelmann's wife had business in Harxbüttel on her son's farm often enough, only she had not looked for advice from the imprisoned except that she had come out with the high countess and the *Beckerse*.

---

1   Presumably this is the mayor, Jürgen Düvel.
2   The baker's wife.

Folio 8

[In Folio 3 Tempel Anneke answers questions about the accusation made by the publican of Harxbüttel, Hans Harves, that she conjured an injury into his leg. In this folio the officials question Hennig Vaddrian, who was said to have brought the accusation from Harves to Tempel Anneke. Tempel Anneke is then confronted with Vaddrian.]

The testimony of Hennig Vaddrian without torture, his confirmation by oath and the subsequent confrontation concerning the *Inquisitionalem* 23. 24. 25. 26. and 27. in *Actis. Num* 2.

The 20th of July *Anno* 1663

Actum in the municipal hall of Hagen

The 20th of July *Anno* 1663

Through the appointed court officers and court magistrates of the municipality of Hagen.

Hennig Vaddrian, Hennig's son, *admonitus de veritate dicenda*, reports that he knows Tempel Anneke well, and that he has called and proclaimed her a witch, *in praesentia*[1] good people, not once but a thousand times. But especially, when recently he wanted to fetch some rams from Tempel Anneke's son's farm, from the shepherd who was there in the house, at the same time he was commanded and ordered by Tempel Hans, Hans Harves, the current publican, to tell Tempel Anneke, how Tempel Hans suspected her, that he had got his lame leg from no one else but from her, and that she was under suspicion of this and should help him so that he would get well again, or he would have to do something else about it. How then the witness said all this to the face of the oftmentioned Tempel Anneke, in the presence of a shoe mender who stayed with her and constantly ate and drank with her on her son's farm. But she answered nothing to that but immediately turned around and went

---

1   "In the presence of."

into the house. And there is a woman in Harxbüttel who is supposed to have the most knowledge about all her dealings.

He presented this his testimony, and that he does not know anything else, he strengthened it with an oath made in person, /: *gravia admonitione de evitando perjurio ejusq. atrocissima poena.* : /

Hereupon the imprisoned Tempel Anneke was questioned once again about the *Articulos Inquisitionales* to be found *Sub Num. Actus* 2, namely about *Inquisitionalem* 23. 24. 25. 26. and 27. and gave her answer to that now as follows:

Ad.

23. *Whether Hennig Vaddrian on the Knochenhauer Street in Hagen didn't once come to her because of an injury like that,*
   Says she saw him at that time when he, Vaddrian, wanted to buy rams on her son's farm, but she didn't know that Vaddrian had come there because of the publican, as she didn't talk with him.

Ad.

24. *Whether Harves didn't let her be told through the same, that he got his ailment through no one else but her,*
   Says, she didn't hear that, otherwise in truth she would have gone to the publican, it shouldn't happen like that, and to be notified with those words.

Ad.

25. *Whether she wasn't threatened, if she wouldn't remove the injury from him, that he would look for help in another place,*
   Says, she didn't hear that, otherwise she would have gone to the publican, and she won't let this happen, she will take this further, one should not put on to someone in this way what he has not done.

Ad.

26. *Whether he didn't add that, if she were innocent, she should come and answer the charge,*
   Says by her living soul she didn't hear that, otherwise she would have gone there.

Hennig Vaddrian is confronted with the imprisoned about these previous four *Inquisitional Articul*, and he said steadfastly to her face that he, as previously testified and sworn to, 1) was caused by the Tempel publican 2) to say to her on the farm /: *right at the time when the now imprisoned was helping the oxherd of Walle to herd a dun-coloured ox off the farm* :/that the publican had his injury from no other than from her, and that 3) if she didn't remove or take the injury away from him, the publican, again, he would look for help in a different place, and 4) if she were innocent, she should come and answer the charge.

Only the imprisoned did not want to admit to that, but countered that she didn't see him, or that she did see him, as she now remembered, nevertheless didn't hear that he spoke to her in this way. And although she stood by this her answer as before, that she did not hear that, even though she did see him that time in the yard, still the witness stands consistently by it that he talked so loudly and openly standing about six steps away from her in the yard, that anyone who might be present in the yard, but more precisely that her son and the shoe mender who were standing close by, could hear enough, since the mentioned shoe mender answered immediately and said, yes, Hans /: *Harves* :/ puts this down to nobody but her.[1]

Ad.

27. *Why did she stay away, and also gave no answer to the butcher,*
   Says she didn't hear this, and Vaddrian said nothing to her, otherwise she would have surely wanted to answer the charge. Even though the witness, Vaddrian, repeated his current testimony and said it again to the face of the imprisoned, that he told her everything that time in her presence, that she could well hear and understand, nevertheless she stood by her denials, and added, if the shoe mender heard this at that time, he acted like a rogue, that he did not tell her, that she could have answered to the charge.

The witness stood consistently by his testimony.

---

[1] It is curious that neither Tempel Anneke's son nor his wife is interrogated, whereas they do look unsuccessfully for the shoe maker. Her son is mentioned again in the testimony of Hennig Roleffes in Folio 18, and elsewhere.

Folio 9

[Hans Isensee was a school master who boarded at the home of Tempel Anneke. He testifies concerning her activities. Another boarder at the farm, an unnamed shoe mender, could not be found.]

Hans Isensee, the children's teacher in Harxbüttel, his statement without torture
The 25th of July *Anno* 1663

Actum in the municipal jail of Hagen

The 25th of July *Anno* 1663

By the honourable Gabriel Oeding, officer of the court, also Otto Theune, magistrate of the court and Johann Pilgram the court scribe.

Hans Isensee of Seershausen in the municipality of Meinerse, now school master in Harxbüttel, residing in a room on Tempel Anneke's son's farm, *admonitus de veritate dicenda*, reports that throughout this past winter in the said place he taught the children, of whom there wasn't more than half a score, and in addition he supported himself with his tailoring. During that time it happened many a day, that 2, 3, 4, and even 5, people,—from everywhere, not only from Brunswick and Campen, but also from other places and from beyond Wolfenbüttel, also on some days none at all—came out to her son's farm and had business at her place. But what they, and one or the other, were seeking for themselves at her place or what kind of advice she gave them, that he didn't know, because every time she went with the people into her room and talked with them.

Further the witness reports, that before this he was in Thune and he stayed around there for about ten years, and had heard / : *but could not say how often or frequently* :/ that it was said of Tempel Anneke, that Tempel Anneke was a sorceress and was thought of as such. Also she had two large books and one small book out of which several pages had been torn. In them base things about chills, about this and that, about horses, and the like, were written there, he could not remember all of it.

He knew nothing more except good day and goodbye, had nothing to do with Anneke, and her things must have helped those people, otherwise they would not have been running after them.

Nota[1] The shoe mender was to be summoned and questioned as well, but because he had already left Harxbüttel 14 days ago, and off to Ribbesbüttel, and after he wasn't tolerated there without showing a testimonial,[2] he moved further away, his testimony has to be omitted.

---

1   "Note."
2   This would be an official letter attesting to his good character.

Folio 10

[This folio contains three letters from the court in Brunswick to the officials in Gifhorn, Campen, and Neubrück, asking that certain witnesses in those jurisdictions report to Brunswick to give evidence. These witnesses are Anna Timmerman, who testifies in Folio 14a, Hille Voge, who testifies in Folio 11, and Hennig Roleffes, who testifies in Folio 18. Also in this folio is the reply from Gifhorn.]

Requisitoriales in subsid.[1] to the regional civil administrator and civil officer of Gifhorn, Herr Andreas Schonberg and Martin Bregen,
civil officer of Campen, Johann Damm
to the civil officer of Neubrück, Johann Gürn
the 3rd *Augustii Anno* 1663

Together with two following documents received,[2]

Nota[3] These three letters were first sent to Herr Mayor Boess, and after they received the seal of the same, they were delivered through the bailiff {...}[4]

Gifhorn

Our greetings and service in friendship first, highly born, powerful and strong also knightly, admired and learned, especially highly honoured gentlemen and reliable friends.

The same are herewith informed in friendship, which will also be known to you yourselves from the local talk of the people, in which way not long ago an old woman from Harxbüttel called Tempel Anneke came under arrest here in Brunswick because of her suspicious divining, and so far it has been inquired into carefully. What came to light amongst other things from the resulting *Actis*, is that the swineherd woman of Bechtsbüttel *N.N.*[5] may carry

---

1 "Request in the service of justice."
2 The first of these two letters, from Gifhorn, is found at the end of this folio. The other, from Campen, is found in Folios 12, 13, and 14.
3 This note was added later at the bottom of the page.
4 The page is cut off at this point.
5 "I am ignorant of the name" (*Nomen Nescio*). This person is in fact Anna Timmerman.

no small knowledge about the said Tempel Anneke's doings and what the same now and then divined for the people. And the said swineherd woman's testimony, also *ratione confrontationis*,[1] is of great importance to us because, in order to send off the same, we would like very much to have the *Acta* completed.

As our request in friendship reaches the honourable, most noble, powerful, also honoured and admired gentlemen, the same will want to lend us a helping hand with this state of affairs, *in subsidium Juris*,[2] and to enjoin and to order the oftmentioned swineherd woman through the power of office, that she should appear here the next coming Saturday morning, God willing, and report to the magistrate of the court, the honourable Otto Theune, in Hagen on Fallersleben Street, for the above mentioned reasons, and that she must testify as much as she knows of the truth at the time.

As well as furthering the beneficial *Justitio*[3] work through this, our citizens as well as the good people of the region reaching far and wide {...}[4]

{...} and at any time we offer to reciprocate

{...} will wish on all sides godly goodwill and protection, given in Brunswick, the 3rd of August *Anno* 1663

Campen

Our greetings in friendship first, knightly, much respected and well-learned, especially most gracious friend.

The same is already aware from the common talk, in which way an old woman from Harxbüttel called Tempel Anneke came to be arrested here because of her suspicious business and divining. Then as it can be seen from the *Inquisition Actis* conducted so far, she not only gave advice regarding dying sheep to the sheep master N. Hoiers when he was still in Harxbüttel but also gave advice to the High Countess of Lehre regarding six missing ducats. And we would very much like to have correct knowledge about that, considering that the imprisoned has at this time without torture only told some of it, but gave no testimony in depth. So our request in friendship and subsidiary petition reaches the civil officer, that he may officially enjoin and order the

---

1 "Record of the confrontation."
2 "In the aid of justice."
3 "Justice."
4 The bottom of the sheet is cut off at this point.

shepherd as well as the High Countess, that they both should appear next Saturday, God willing, early in the day and report to the magistrate of the court, the honourable Otto Theune, on Fallersleben Street, and give true testimony about what had been revealed and advised to them by Tempel Anneke. And this will aid the prevention of further fraud and injury both to our fellow citizens and people in the country far and wide. We are looking forward to the subsidiary help of the civil officer, and we make the proper offer to reciprocate, in the same and different situations.

May the Almighty protect you.

Done and given in Brunswick the 3rd of August *Anno* 1663

To the civil officer in friendship
Court officers and magistrates of the municipality of Hagen in that very place.

Neubrück

Our greeting in friendship first, knightly, much respected and well-learned, especially highly honoured gentleman and friend.

We are not withholding from the same, which we believe is also known to him from local talk, in which way an old woman from Harxbüttel called Tempel Anneke came to be under arrest here in Brunswick, because of her suspicious business and divining. As it is found in the *Inquisition Actis* conducted so far, that Hennig Roleffes of Wenden is acquainted with her because of this, and therefore we would very much like have a report, what her advice and help had been to him. So our request reaches the civil officer to offer us a hand *in subsidium Juris*, that he may officially enjoin and order said Hennig Roleffes, that he should appear the next coming Saturday, God willing, early in the day and report to the magistrate of the court, the honourable Otto Theune, on Fallersleben Street, and to report as much as he knows. Through this we further the esteemed law, and many a respectable person is protected from fraud and injury. Anticipating action helpful to us, we are willing to reciprocate in the same situation.

Given in Brunswick under our court seal, the 3rd of August *Anno* 1663
To the civil officer in friendship
court officers and magistrates of the municipality of Hagen in that very place

Received from the ducal office of Gifhorn

The 5th *Augusti*, 1663

The letter well received here from the joint court officers and magistrates of the municipality of Hagen, will be certified herewith, and should order in the desired manner, that the named person should appear next Saturday before the court magistrate, in the aid of justice

Gifhorn, the 4th *Augusti* 1663
From the ducal office
B.[1]

---

1   Martin Bregen, civil officer. For more discussion of the officers involved in the trial, see pp. xxxv-xxvii.

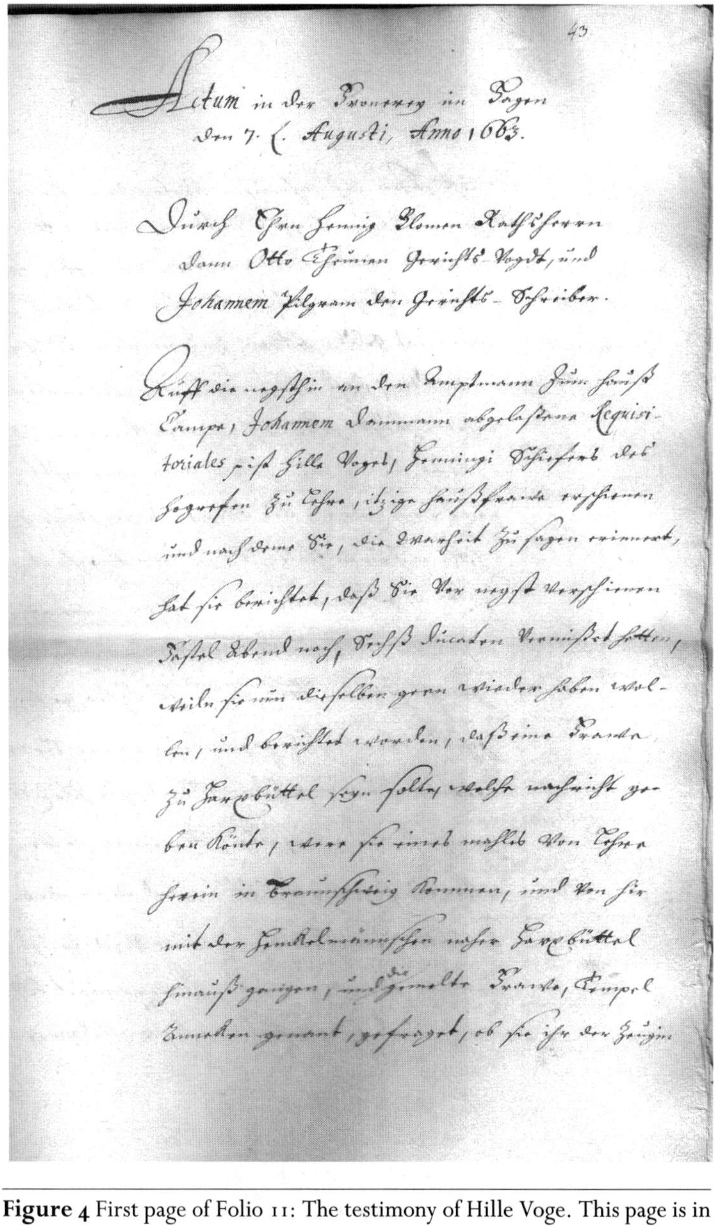

Figure 4 First page of Folio 11: The testimony of Hille Voge. This page is in the hand of the court scribe, Johann Pilgram, who recorded all of the testimony given in Hagen before the Lower Court officers. It contains the first part of the testimony of Hille Voge, the High Countess of Lehre.

Folio 11

[This folio contains the sworn testimony of Hille Voge, High Countess of Lehre, whose name first appears in Folio 2, and her confrontation with Tempel Anneke.]

August 7 1663

Frau Hille Voge, the wedded housewife of the High Count of Lehre, her statement without torture and its verbal affirmation together with the subsequent confrontation

The 7th *Augusti Anno* 1663

Actum in the municipal jail of Hagen
7th Augusti Anno 1663

By the Honourable Hennig Blome, officer of the court, also Otto Theune, magistrate of the court, and Johann Pilgram, the court scribe.

Following the recent *Requisitionalis*[1] given to the civil officer of Campen, Johann Damm, Hille Voge, present housewife of Hennig Schiefer, High Count of Lehre, appeared. After she was reminded to tell the truth, she reported that before the previous Shrove Tuesday, six ducats were missing. Because she very much wanted to have those back, and she was told that there was a woman in Harxbüttel who could give information, on one occasion she came from Lehre into Brunswick, and from here later out to Harxbüttel with the *Henkelmännische*,[2] and there asked the said woman, called Tempel Anneke, whether she couldn't tell her, the witness, or divine, since she had lost six ducats in her house in Lehre and that she very much wanted them back. Whereupon Tempel Anneke replied to her in her hall, the witness's blood relatives had the money, it was still under her own roof in her house, it would reappear, she would do that. The witness should just search in her house in the morning for eight days in a row, she also asked for a Taler from the witness, and so the money should return. But when the eight

---

days had passed, and the witness had searched thoroughly every morning in her house in Lehre, but didn't find anything, she went again to Tempel Anneke in Harxbüttel / : *because the same had already got half a Taler* : / and the other half Taler was later made good in flax by the wife of the witness's brother, Zacharias Voge. And she told her that she had searched each morning but had found nothing yet. To this Tempel Anneke replied that she couldn't get the money back so quickly, but it would need time. She stood by what she had said, that the money should return. When the farmer wanted to buy grain, he would have to uncover the ducats, and this was everything that Tempel Anneke told the witness. With that she left the same, and remained with her previous belief, until on the aforementioned Shrove Tuesday her husband, the High Count, found them again unexpectedly four weeks after he had missed them, in his pants pocket under his letters where they had slid, when for other reasons and because the pants needed mending he unpacked his pockets. The witness knew nothing more to say. She was supposed to and wanted to strengthen all this with her oath, which was omitted this time because of her heavy foot,[1] and she declared that what she said was the truth, so help her God.

Hereupon the prisoner, Tempel Anneke, was interrogated again concerning *Inquisitionalem* 31, 32, and 33, formulated amongst others in *Actis Num.* 2. And because she stood by her earlier testimony, the witness was confronted with her. And after Tempel Anneke again still stood by her currently given answers to the above mentioned *Articulos* in *Actis Num.* 3, she[2] said the same words specified above, clearly and unafraid to her face. And in spite of Tempel Anneke standing by her previous answers *ad Artos*[3] 31, 32, and 33, through her telling of the circumstances, the witness nevertheless brought the same to where she[4] said for the first time that she forgot it. But afterwards the prisoner was hemmed in such a way, because she could not gainsay that she had got for half of it money and for the other half flax, that she could no longer deny but had to confess that she had given the witness such advice, that she was supposed to look carefully in the mornings, and that the money should come back, because it was still in the house.

J. Pilgram
court scribe

---

1   Presumably an injury of some kind.
2   Hille Voge.
3   "With respect to the articles."
4   Tempel Anneke.

Folio 12

[Following upon the letter from Brunswick to Campen in Folio 10, this letter from Johann Damm of Campen requests that the court in Brunswick also question Tempel Anneke about a woman from Essenrode. The list of questions appears in Folio 13.]

Requisitoriales of the civil officer of Campen[1]
including attached previous question points[2]
about which Tempel Anneke is to be interrogated *in subsidium*

Received the 7th *Augusti Anno* 1663

To the most honourable, much respected and well-learned officers of the court and magistrates of the municipality of Hagen in the city of Brunswick, especially very generous, cherished friends.

Most honourable, much respected and most wise, especially most gracious, honoured friends. After I learned from your letter that an old woman from Harxbüttel, called Tempel Anneke, was taken into custody there because of her suspicious business and divining, I ask officially, that you will question the mentioned imprisoned about the enclosed *interrogatoria*,[3] and communicate her testimony to me. On the basis of all of the events I offer to support you here in return. In this way, surrendering to the care of God, I remain,

your willing servant
Johann Joachim Damm

Campen the 6.Aug. *Anno* 1663

---

1   This cover is written over top of the cover to Folio 13.
2   These questions are in Folio 13.
3   "Questions."

Folio 13

[These are the questions that Johann Damm of Campen wishes to be put to Tempel Anneke. The questions are incorporated into Folio 21.]

Interrogatoria[1] about which *Captiva* is to be interrogated.

These *interrogatoria* are put together under the *inquisitional articul sub num. Act* 21.[2]

Interrogatoria about which Tempel Anneke is to be interrogated.

1. Whether a woman from Essenrode came to see her about half a year ago, who had a man who ran away from her, and she attached herself again to the former toll collector of Lehre, Heinrich Weber, and wanted to have the same back again,

2. Whether the said loose woman from Essenrode didn't ask her to give her advice so that she could win the former toll collector,

3. Whether she then gave her something she should administer to the toll collector, so that he could not keep away from her,

4. What kind of things were they, and in which way was she supposed to administer them to the said toll collector,

5. How long ago was it that she gave her advice,

6. How was that supposed to influence him and operate on him.

Tempel Anneke must be questioned about all *Articul.*

---

1   These questions were originally attached to the letter from Campen in Folio 12.
2   This note is added in the margin, presumably later by the Hagen officials. See questions 29 to 31 in Folio 21.

Folio 14a

[This is the testimony of Anna Timmerman, who is first mentioned in Folio 10. Her story forms the basis of much questioning of Tempel Anneke in Folios 21 and 22, and her further testimony is recorded in Folio 39.]

Statement without torture of Anna Timmermann, wife of Hans Wolter, swineherd of Bechtsbüttel
The 8th *Augustii Anno* 1663

Actum in the municipal jail of Hagen, the 8th *Augustii Anno* 1663
By the officers of the court and magistrates of the municipality of Hagen.

Upon the *subsidial*[1] letter sent from the court here to the office of the principality of Gifhorn, Anna Timmerman, the wedded housewife of Hans Wolter, current swineherd of Bechtsbüttel, appeared and reported, *gravia admonitione de veritate dicenda*, that some 8 years ago her husband was a swineherd in Harxbüttel, and that besides him she stayed there herself and lived there with her children. It happened one time, that the witness's son, about 8 years old, was playing with the Commander's son in front of the house in the sand box, and Tempel Anneke came by and grabbed the witness's son by the head, and as the said Commander's son—named Heinrich Jochim, who now serves as a farm hand with Jürgen Roleffes of Harxbüttel—reported, she spun him around, so that the boy fell to the ground, and he started and said to Tempel Anneke, "You old whore, go drink your beer." But she waved with her hand and said at the same time, "Now you'll regret that." Before three days had passed, on the fourth day at noon, a cow from the witness's animals turned ill and was dead three hours later. Fourteen days later the witness had a cow become ill, and it was dead the next day following that. Again 14 days later she had a cow fall in the heather and stay dead. After four weeks passed, a one-and-a-half year old pig became ill at noon and was dead by evening. But other people's animals neither became ill nor died, and the witness couldn't say that it came from Tempel Anneke, she also couldn't say that it didn't come from her, except were it not that after the boy, as reported above, insulted Tempel Anneke, soon the misfortune hit her animals alone and it didn't hurt

---

1   "Subsidiary, supporting."

other people's animals. She submitted everything to the authorities, at that time the witness was unable to raise or keep animals. Yes, when they moved away from Harxbüttel six years ago, they had only one cow left, which was fresh and healthy in the morning, but by the time they got to the Harxbüttel heather towards another common the cow first fell ill {...}, was also brought ill to Beienrode, and was found dead in the morning.

After the witness's animals, as mentioned, fell one after the other, her son became ill, the left leg of the same became swollen thick as a head, so that he also could not rest or sleep day and night because of the pain, but instead cried out terribly from it. On one occasion while the witness and her husband were not at home Tempel Anneke came unexpectedly to the sick child, the already mentioned son, in the house, and gave the same a yellow pear. But the son didn't want to accept the pear from her nor eat it, because of that the mentioned Tempel Anneke left it on the mantle in a kettle. Now when the witness's daughter, then about ten years old but now passed away, came home, and didn't know that Tempel Anneke had put the pear in the kettle, /: *as the pear was in the kettle as if it were specially saved* :/ the daughter gave the oftmentioned yellow pear to her sick brother, and the sick boy ate it up except for a small bit, which was left and was all black to look at. Soon he got bad pains and suffering low in his body, and not only was his lower body bloated, but also the swelling above his genitals /: *salva venia* :/ was lying so thickly that it hung over half his body. Now when the boy was in such bad shape, word was sent to Tempel Anneke that she should help the boy. When she came she sat down, looked at the child and said "Be quiet, you won't die of this." She came in this way once or three times and she accepted offerings, three Ortstaler, ham and sausages, what was given to her. One time during the illness, which lasted 14 weeks, the witness was away. Tempel Anneke came to the witness's house, and she gave her husband to understand that he should carry the sick child into the garden behind the house onto the tilled soil, which was dug up by the witness about two days before, to place the same on his back and to stretch out his hands and feet. Then Tempel Anneke approached and planted something, which she would know and understand best, at his hands, feet and also at his head. Then the child—because of great pain and whimpering, and also one leg was already completely bent and couldn't be straightened—couldn't keep lying on the tilled soil longer than it took to do the planting. Then the father had to pick him up again right away because of the pain and carry him to his bed. Because it had been going on with the child for 14 weeks, as mentioned, the witness's husband

[51]

finally became impatient. And when he came in from the common in the evening and saw that Tempel Anneke was still in his house sitting by the fire, he started and said, "How is it? Will you help him or not?" He then jumped in and grabbed the battle axe from the wall, and the witness had no doubt, had she not been afraid of her husband's intense anger, and stepped between them and screamed, that he would have cut an arm off Tempel Anneke's body. Hereupon Tempel Anneke jumped out of the front door and didn't say one word. She also got out of Harxbüttel, and didn't return for nine weeks.

Following this they sent an Ortstaler to Herr Heinrich in Garbsen. He sent the boy some ointment for 6*g*. and returned 3*g*. Thereupon, because of the ointment five bones fell from his left knee. And God helped him so far that he recovered and is now a boy of 16 years, but one can still see nevertheless that he had five holes in his knee, and the knee cap is gone completely, except for a little piece that still hangs down from it.

Folio 14b

[This is the reply from Johann Gürn of Neubrück to the letter recorded in Folio 10. Gürn included with this letter the testimonies of Christoff Meinicke, the miller of Neubrück, which is contained in Folio 15, and that of Christoff Rieckmann, contained in Folio 16.]

Received the 8th of August 1663

To the knightly, much respected and well-learned, highly honoured gentlemen and very cherished friends.

Brunswick

Most knightly, much respected and well-learned court officers and magistrates of the municipality of Hagen in Brunswick.

I have rightfully received what was sent to me by the same, and immediately enjoined Hennig Roleffes of Wenden *in subsidium juris* to appear the next Saturday early in the day at the requested place, and to report what he knows about Tempel Anneke. Not wanting to bypass my highly respected gentlemen, I am giving news through a desire for cooperation, how far the woman who was brought into legal custody by you carried on here in this jurisdiction, and what occurred through that.[1] Enclosed for your receipt are also the roots with which she defrauded the local miller. And should it be necessary to call the same in this matter to Brunswick in person, I am offering, according to the given subsidiary citation, to urge him amongst others to report there, which is useful for the furtherance of beneficial justice as is our due.

And I recommend the same to godly protection.

District office of Neubrück, the 5th of August, *Anno* 1663

---

1   The news referred to here are the testimonies of Christoff Meinicke and Christoff Rieckmann, in Folios 15 and 16, which were originally enclosed with this letter to Brunswick.

My highly respected gentlemen, and very valued friends,
at all times ready to be of service,
Johann Gürn

Folio 15

[This is the testimony of Christoff Meinicke, sent with the letter of Folio 14b. The phrase "put on the wheel" implies that Meinicke was tortured.]

Actum in the district office of Neubrück
the 3rd of August *Anno* 1663

After it was established otherwise, in what way a horribly notorious woman, called Tempel Anneke, arrested a few weeks ago in Brunswick, this year promised the miller of this jurisdiction that she wanted to help him, how he could always have loads of mill customers. About this the miller, Christoff Meinicke, is summoned, and was put on the wheel. Who reports that he must confess that the said old woman—now in custody after the same was sued here by Hennig Roleffes from Wenden on the charge of witchcraft—came to him in the mill. And because he mentioned among other things that there was no profit in this worrisome time, that this woman answered, "Don't worry, I will help you, that you will get enough flour to mill, yes, so much that the people will fight each other over it." What he now asked out of pure simplemindedness was, "What will you want to give me." She pulled out half a loaf of bread and a dried apple, several very small roots, godlessly ordered him to sew these[1] in his clothes, and to keep them warm all the time, to wear them on his body. But this he didn't do, especially after he then searched within himself and was afraid of sin. He threw these roots in a {...} hole on the post in his room, from which he sought them out again today, and as soon as he came to get them, he found them unexpectedly, as he had not thought that they would still be there. Concerning what Tempel Anneke said, that mill customers would fight amongst each other, this more than came about, even though the milling business wasn't strongly advanced by that. Furthermore the miller reports that at that time he had a mill labourer, who had never in his life seen the suspected old witch woman, even less heard about her, yet she said to the same when she came face to face with him, that he had got a loose woman pregnant, and she would come soon to bring him the child and thereby would urge him to marry her. Only he should not do that, that she liked to drink excessively and was furthermore Catholic. Then after that everything happened and was true.

---

1   I.e., the roots.

Folio 16

[This is the testimony of Christoff Rieckmann, sent with the letter of Folio 14b.]

Summary of local district office *Protocollo*
What Christoff Rieckmann testified regarding Tempel Anneke

The report of Christoff Rieckmann, of Thune, done in the district office of Neubrück the 5th of August 1663

Actum in the district office of Neubrück
the 5th of August *Anno* 1663

Accordingly Christoff Rieckmann cottager of this jurisdiction in the village of Thune, languished in the summer a year ago with a serious illness, and there together with his wife and children, as well as all who were in their house, they were lying down badly stricken. Then together they lost[1] their limbs, like hands, feet and more, and then a heaviness came to their heads so that nobody knew what they were doing. We also found out that, after he came upon the thought that this might be witchcraft, the same was believed to have hired the same Tempel Anneke. So we wanted to summon him today and interrogate him about this, who testified that he must confess that he and his own had been healed by this woman, and at the same time was told by her, that this illness was given to him by evil people. After certain means were used, the very person who was guilty of that should soon appear at Rieckmann's house to borrow something. And even though this happened, that someone from the neighbourhood appeared in person, still, he, the said Rieckmann, could not on the strength of this speak ill of someone. And it could as easily be this person as another who did it to him through harmful means. With that he finished his testimony, *actum ut Supra.*[2]

Note: The contents of Folio 17 have been re-numbered as Document A and moved to p. 3. See p. xxiv of the Introduction.

---

1 The meaning here might be "lost use of" their limbs.
2 "The proceeding as above."

Folio 18

[This folio contains the sworn testimony of Hennig Roleffes of Wenden and the record of his confrontation with Tempel Anneke concerning her answers in Folio 3, which were first requested in Folio 10. Roleffes's testimony is often grammatically convoluted, and it is difficult to make complete sense of some parts of it.]

Hennig Roleffes's repeated statement without torture, and collateral statement including confrontation concerning the extracted *Articulos* contained here, and questions formed from the collateral report.

The 8th *Augusti Anno* 1663

Actum in the municipal jail of Hagen, the 8th *Augustii Anno* 1663

By all the persons of the court of the municipality of Hagen

In accordance with the given *Requisitoriales*, Hennig Roleffes of Wenden appeared, the same was presented again, clearly and carefully according to the letter, with his testimony without torture in *Actis Num* 1 of the 25th of this past June, and not only did he consistently stand by it, what he testified on his own and his brother's behalf, but he also remembered and further now stated, that Tempel Anneke appeared at his home on a Sunday morning last fall, and gave him to understand that it had been sent into his brother Jürgen Roleffes's farm, and if the witness wanted to change something about it, as it would come to help him, she wanted to send it out again. At the same time Tempel Anneke thought and said, that if her son Hans Kage of Harxbüttel had been willing to give her something on which to booze or live, none of his animals should have died, /: *namely the two calves and one cow, which died away so shortly one after the other* :/ But he gave her nothing, nor wanted to hire her for that, instead he let the *Schwensche*[1] of Wenden be fetched for that, who was supposed to look at the blood. He also wanted to have it that he must add something to it /: *specifically from the animals, like the others.* :/ Even though the *Schwensche* studied the blood, Tempel Anneke apparently knew better, she

---

1 A woman's name.

thought herself to be master of the *Schwensche*, that is, as the witness explains, she could do more than the *Schwensche* and the *Eblersche*.

And because she wanted to do it, because she wanted to bring it about, for the *Schwensche* to go to Vordorf and fetch the *Eblersche*, and that both should come to Harxbüttel.

Further the witness remembered from this, that Tempel Anneke said a year ago to the current publican Hans Harves, how he, the witness, heard this with his own ears, that he would not miss the cow, and the cock—to which she was throwing bread in the farmyard at that time—he would keep on the farm, but the hens would perish. Further the witness remembers how when he was still a boy of 12 that Tempel Anneke had been accused by her own brother Hennig Roleffes[1] because she had bewitched his cows, and the same had wanted to have her arrested and burnt. However, Tempel Anneke took herself away. And after her brother died and already 9 years had passed, she came back. Because the brother's animals were so bewitched, the old *Martensche*[2] from Wenden, from whom Tempel Anneke was supposed to have learned her arts as well as from her godmother, had to come and help the animals again, by sitting on the bewitched cows and mounting the same. But the witness didn't know what she had done. And both the brothers of Tempel Anneke, Heinrich Roleffes of Wenden and Valentin Roleffes of Rohe, could bear witness to this. In this way the witness was able to strengthen with his oath what he had earlier testified and what had been clearly put before him again, and also what else he had now stated further, to be the real truth and that he wasn't aware of anything else, *gravia admonitione de evitando perjuro ejusq. atrocissima poena.*

After this Tempel Anneke is questioned again about the *Inquisitionalis Articulos* contained in *Actis Num.* 2, specifically about *Artm.* numbers 44, 45, 46, 47, and 52, and answered to each as follows:

Ad.

44. *Whether she didn't offer to help them when dying befell the sheep in Harxbüttel,*
Says, the shepherd wanted to run away, because the sheep had dropsy and other ailments, so she said, one has to look into how to use things. Also she gave the people blackberries, salt, oak leaves, field hops and wild sage. All of this was boiled by the *Schaffmeisterse* in the house of

---

1 This is a different person from the Hennig Roleffes giving testimony here.
2 A woman's name.

the son of *Inquisitin* and was given to the other sheep. At the same time that the aforementioned herbs were cooking, part of the dead butchered sheep was burned to powder, and was mixed in with them.

Ad.

45. *Whether she didn't bring the dying amongst the sheep through sorcery,*
Negat iterum.[1]

Ad.

46. *How, and by which means, did she want to help the sheep,*
Says as just now *ad.* 44 *Inquisitionalem.*

Ad.

47. *Whether she didn't burn a sheep from the herd to powder in the oven, cooked something in a kettle, and administered it to the sheep,*
Says, the *Schaffmeisterse* burned the dead sheep from the herd to powder, and *Inquisitin* gave her this advice, because *Inquisitin* had seen this before from a sheep master at the Niendorff monestary, the other side of Gardelegen.

Ad.

48. *Whether she didn't learn such things from the Evil Enemy,*
Says as *ad proxe praecedentem Inquisitionalem*, and adds, that comes from God the Lord, that things are used. Must everything only come from the Evil Enemy.

Ad.

52. *Whether he [Hennig Roleffes of Wenden] didn't give her 3 Taler and a goose, so that she should help him again,*
Says it wasn't 3 whole Taler, but only 2 Taler. 16g., and the goose was eaten at the house of the Commander, and she didn't see the same, also didn't eat from it, because she came too slowly.

After this Tempel Anneke is further questioned and after consideration the witness is confronted with her:

---

1 "Denied again."

1. *Whether last fall on a Sunday morning Inquisitin didn't talk to Hennig Roleffes*
   and put forward, that it had been sent to the farm of his brother Jürgen Roleffes, and
   if the witness wanted to help and change that, she wanted to send it out again,
   Says, no.

Hereupon the witness is confronted with *Inquisitin* and said consistently to
the same to her face that she talked with him about this and put it forward
as reported, only *Inquisitin* didn't want to confess. But as the witness stood
consistently by his testimony, she finally said, yes, that was true. But when
she was questioned why it was true now, even though she had said no before,
she answered, because the witness said so and swore to it, it had to be true.
When they now responded to her, that she had to confess herself and tell the
truth, otherwise her yes could not be written down as the truth and a legal
confession, she answered again and said, yes, yes, she had done that. This
her answer appeared to the court officials as if *Inquisitin* had said that out of
indignant anger, which she felt about the confrontation with her neighbour.

Further questioned:

2. *Whether Inquisitin didn't say, if her son gave her something so that she was able*
   to live or more accurately to booze, that none of his animals should die, but now
   he could have it, now he fetched the Schwensche from Wenden for that,
   Says, no.

Hereupon the witness is again confronted with *Inquisitin*, and even though
he told all this consistently to her face, she still stood consistently by her
denials. Now as the witness still stood consistently by his testimony and with
this contended that, on the wishes of the court officials of Brunswick, his civil
official had ordered that he had to tell the truth, finally *Inquisitin* gave as her
reply and said: that this time one should write down yes, because the witness
would / : God save us : / lie or perjure the horns off the Devil.

Further questioned:

3. *Whether Inquisitin didn't say that she was the master of the Schwensche of*
   Wenden,
   Says, yes, with blessings with brookweed blood and chick blood, and
   with bloating and pox she was the better or master of the *Schwensche*.

Because the blessing happens with three words, approximately, as when one gives a blessing, one wears an apron, or if it is a man who wants to bless, a hat, and says: "John and the Holy Evangelists, they pluck a branch in Paradise," with that they blessed the thick blood and the thin blood, /: *the thick blood was the chick blood, the thin blood was the brookweed blood* :/ and with these words they say, "in the name of the Father, the Son and the Holy Spirit."

4. *Whether Inquisitin didn't say, when she wanted to do this and wanted to bring it about that the Schwensche should go to the Eblersche of Vordorf, and both should come to Harxbüttel?*
Says, yes, one should write down that she said yes. And even though she was reminded to watch what she was saying, she still stood by it, one should write down yes, because the witness consistently said to her face, that she said the reported words not once but several times.

5. *Whether it isn't true, that Inquisitin once threw something to the cock in the Tempel yard in Harxbüttel and with that said, "The cock shall stay around, the chickens are gone, yet it is better than the cows, that is, than if the cows were wasted."*
Says, yes, because the chickens died, but the chicks with them suffered, for them she had sprinkled rye to eat, which she had earlier mixed with ashes and salt, and had put it through a broom in her lap three times, because it is customary to give that to calves when they suffer or feel pain.

Folio 19

[This is the testimony of Tempel Anneke's brother, Heinrich Roleffes of Wenden.]

The statement without torture of Heinrich Roleffes, the imprisoned Tempel Anneke's own brother
The 12th *Augusti Anno* 1663

Actum in the municipal jail of Hagen
the 12th of August *Anno* 1663

By the appointed persons of the court of the municipality of Hagen

For the purpose of the *Requisitorialibus*[1] of the Lower Court, recently made to the civil officer of Neubrück, Johann Gürn, Heinrich Roleffes of Wenden, the brother of the *Inquisitin* Tempel Anneke, appeared as well, and after the usual reminder reported that about his sister, he didn't know what she had done, because he hadn't seen it, only that when something happened, the people accused his sister with venom, that she committed wrongs with the animals. *Inquisitin* can best know, he couldn't say anything about it, also he couldn't protect her. And it often happened that everyone was fed up with *Inquisitin*, and that hasn't changed to this day.

---

1   "Request."

Folio 20

[This is the sworn testimony of Heinrich Cordes of Wenden, who was first questioned in September, 1662, as recorded in Document B. Following his testimony Tempel Anneke is questioned further about the same events and is confronted with Cordes.]

The undertaken confrontation of Heinrich Cordes, the carpenter from Wenden, with the imprisoned Tempel Anneke, concerning the *Protocollum*[1] to be found collected in *Actis Num.* 15.[2]

The 12th *Augusti Anno* 1663

Actum in the municipal jail of Hagen
The 12th *Augusti Anno* 1663

By the appointed court officers and magistrates of the municipality of Hagen

When Heinrich Cordes, carpenter from Wenden, appeared in accordance with the *requisitoriales* recently made by the Lower Court of Hagen, he was interrogated about the *Sub Num Actorum* contained in the *Protocollum*, sent by the civil officer of Neubrück, Johann Gürn in *Actis Num* 15. The same was put before him again clearly word by word, and because the witness Cordes stood consistently by it, and he remembers nothing further, except that he now remembers, that his child had not been crying and calling for two days, but only on the morning when Tempel Anneke left, and the following night. Then the next day he sent right away to Tempel Anneke, and, as recorded, the child's condition improved, where the fellow Christoff Jürgens had been his messenger on that occasion and had then gone to Tempel Anneke to meet her. Except whether his child's suffering at that time had come from Tempel Anneke, and went away again, the witness could really not say. Only what had happened and what he had reported at the office, and what had been read to

---

1 "Record."
2 The document referred to here, which was filed in Folio 15, has been moved to Document B because it predates the events described in Folio 15.

him again clearly now, that was the truth, he didn't know more or differently. In this way he was then able to strengthen this his testimony, *gravia admonitione de evitando perjurio ejusq. atrocissima poena*, with an oath.

Hereupon Tempel Anneke is introduced and questioned:

1. *Whether about a year ago now she didn't come to Heinrich Cordes's bed and said to the same, that there was a mandrake present in his house, that wanted to move away from him,*

   Says, yes, but what kind of thing is that supposed to be, she had never in her life seen a mandrake, had also never heard of one. And *Inquisitin* found this question almost ridiculous. When the witness was now confronted with her about this *articul*, and said consistently and carefully to her face, that she came at that time to his bed and talked about a mandrake, as reported, and so that the same must stay she wanted half a Taler, she did in fact confess that she was at Christoff Jürgens's and had drunk with the same, but she admitted nothing about the mandrake or what else she had said. But when the witness put it to her that he was not after her and also wished her no ill, only he had to say what was the truth, which was no different from what he had testified and sworn to, *Inquisitin* confessed, that she had now thought about it again, and it was true that she came to his bed and said there was a mandrake in his house that wanted to leave. Only she meant no harm, had also never seen a mandrake in her life.

Inquisitin is questioned further:

2. *Whether she didn't say to Heinrich Cordes, that if he wanted to give her half a Taler, then the mandrake would not move out, because she could make it so that it had to stay,*

   Says, yes. And even though the witness[1] was reminded to honour God the Lord and to tell the truth, and not to deny until she was sufficiently persuaded, because then, as it appeared so far to the officers of the court, she had said yes much more from bitterness than from a love for the truth, still she stood consistently by it, and answered this question now as before with yes.

---

1   I.e., Tempel Anneke.

Hereupon *Inquisitin* was questioned in the absence of the witness specifically: how could she bring it about, that a mandrake must stay? To that she answered, when you bury Christmas Rose and aloe in a small cloth in the name of God under a house sill, so that it could not harden, a mandrake could not move away. And this she had learned from Hans Kükenüss of Thune /: *Zum Zaune*[1] :/ because when he was alive he had one time sat in the pub, and as he was teased about it by the farmers sitting around him, he gave this advice. *Inquisitin* had heard that then, otherwise she knows nothing more about it.

Questioned further:

3. *Whether she didn't do harm to Heinrich Cordes's child so that it cried and shouted,*
   Says, no.

4. *Whether she didn't answer Christoff Jürgens, when he came about Heinrich Cordes's child to her and threatened her, that Cordes wanted to hit her arms and legs crooked and lame, and she said:"Be on your way, there is nothing wrong with the boy,"*
   Says, yes, she told Jürgens to go home and said, "Be on your way, there is nothing wrong with the child, give him lots of chalk and saffron, he has stomach worms."

Now even though it was to presented to *Inquisitin* that the child turned better when the messenger came to her, she still did not want to say anything else, other than what she has now testified *ad Artm* 4.

---

1 The reference here is unclear: from what follows, it may perhaps refer to a pub or an inn.

Folio 21

[Based on the evidence collected in Folios 5 through 20, the Higher Court here formulates a new set of questions upon which to interrogate Tempel Anneke. Her answers appear in Folio 22.]

Further *inquisitionalis*, concerning which the imprisoned is to be questioned, and confronted if necessary.

Further *inquisitionalis*, concerning which the imprisoned is to be questioned, and confronted if necessary.

1. Whether she knows Hans Wolter, current swineherd in Bechtsbüttel and his wife,

2. Whether they lived in Harxbüttel eight years ago,

3. Whether *Inquisitin* knew his child, a boy, eight years ago,

4. Whether, while he was playing one time with the son of the Commander, she didn't grab the same by the head and spin him around,

5. Whether the boy didn't fall to the ground,

6. Whether he didn't call her an old whore,

7. Whether thereupon she didn't wave with her hand saying, "You'll regret that, before three days are over,"

8. Whether upon the 4th day one of the herder's cattle didn't take ill and die,

9. Whether 14 days afterwards one of the cows of the same didn't take ill and fall over in the heather,

10. Whether 4 weeks later one of the herder's pigs didn't fall ill and die,

11. Whether it isn't true that no one else's animals died,

12. Whether when the herder moved away 6 years ago one more cow didn't take ill on the way and die in Beienrode,

13. Whether the imprisoned didn't do all that to the animals, that they died, and how and by what means did she do it,

14. Whether in the end she didn't bewitch the aforementioned son of the herder, so that his left leg swelled up very thickly,

15. Whether she didn't come to the sick child's house and give him a yellow pear,

16. Whether she didn't put the pear on the mantle in a pot, because the sick boy wouldn't accept it,

17. What did she put into this pear that made the inside look all black,

18. Whether she didn't prepare the pear through witchcraft in such a way that the sick boy got severe pains from it low in his body,

19. Whether she didn't make it so that the lower body swelled from this pear,

20. Whether a messenger wasn't sent to her to help the boy,

21. Whether she didn't come and say, "Be quiet, you won't die from this,"

22. Whether *Inquisitin* didn't give the witness's husband to understand that he should carry the sick child to the garden onto the turned soil behind the house,

23. Whether on *Inquisitin*'s instructions he didn't have to lie on his back and stretch his hands and feet,

24. Whether she didn't step up and plant something by the child's hands and feet and also by the head, what was it and what was it for,

25. Whether the swineherd of Bechtsbüttel didn't find her sitting by the fire one evening when he came home,

26. Whether he didn't start in at her, "How is it, will you help him up, or will you let him lie,"

27. Whether he didn't grab the battle axe from the wall and wanted to strike *Inquisitin* with it,

28. Whether she didn't jump away then, and stayed away from Harxbüttel a whole 9 weeks,

29. Whether half a year ago a woman from Essenrode didn't come to her,

30. Whether the same woman didn't ask *Inquisitin* for advice, how she could get the former toll collector[1] in marriage,

31. Whether she didn't give her something that she was to administer to the toll collector, what was it, and what effect should it have on him, also how did it turn out,

32. Whether 9 years ago in Neubrück she didn't get completely drunk with Stoffel Jürgens at master Heinrich Cordes's, as in act. N. 20,[2]

33. Whether at the same time she didn't come to Heinrich Cordes's bed, as in N. 20,

34. Whether she didn't say there was a mandrake in his house that wanted to move away,

35. Whether she didn't demand half a Taler, to make it so that it had to stay,

36. Whether she didn't that same day bewitch the five year old child of Heinrich Cordes,

---

1   Heinrich Weber.
2   "Proceeding number 20."

37. Whether she didn't bring it about through witches's art, that a black thing appeared to the child, that wanted to get the child,

38. What kind of thing it was, and whether it wasn't her lover the Evil Enemy,

39. Whether Cordes didn't threaten her through Stoffel Jürgens that she should take this away from the child again, or he will have her dealt with another way,

40. Whether upon hearing these threatening words she didn't remove it from the child again and said through Stoffel Jürgens: "Stoffel, there is nothing wrong with the boy,"

41. Whether she didn't promise the miller, Christoff Meinicke, that he would get so many customers that they would fight each other for his milling,

42. Whether she didn't give him several dried roots for that, what kind of roots they were, and from whom she got the same,

43. Whether she didn't order him to sew the roots in his clothes and to keep them warm,

44. Whether she didn't say to the miller's helper that he had made a woman pregnant, who will bring him the child some day soon,

45. How did she know that, whether it wasn't her lover the Evil Enemy who revealed it to her,

46. Whether she added that the woman liked to get drunk and was Catholic,

47. Whether she didn't help Christoff Rieckmann of Thune as well as his wife and children with a serious illness. What kind of illness was it, and how did she cure the same, what did she use for it and who taught her,

48. Whether she didn't say that the person who had given them the illness should soon come to Rieckmann's house to borrow something,

49. Whether she didn't do sorcery to the said person so that the person had to come there, how she had done that, and who had taught her.

Folio 22

[These are Tempel Anneke's replies to the questions in Folio 21. As in Folio 3, the questions do not appear in the original records but are repeated here for convenience.]

Reply given by the imprisoned Tempel Anneke to the further *Inquisitionales* drawn up in *Act. Num* 21, the 24th *Augusti Anno* 1663

Actum in the municipal jail of Hagen
the 24th *Augusti Anno* 1663

By the honourable Gabriel Oeding, official of the court, also Johann Velhagen and Otto Theune, both magistrates of the court, and Johann Pilgram the court scribe.

On the received order of the E.E. most esteemed council given once more, the imprisoned Tempel Anneke was questioned about the further *Inquisitionales* drawn up in *Actis Num.* 21 and has given her specific answer to each one, as written down here *formalibus verbis*:

1. *Whether she knows Hans Wolter, current swineherd in Bechtsbüttel, and his wife,*
   Says, yes, knows them very well.

2. *Whether they lived in Harxbüttel eight years ago,*
   Says nothing, or she just didn't know how long ago it was that he herded the swine in Harxbüttel, it has been a good long time now.

3. *Whether Inquisitin knew his child, a boy, eight years ago,*
   Says, yes, that was a *Jünike* /: *a little boy* :/ was named Curdt, and she believed that the same was still alive. Because his father was still in Harxbüttel before the time of the plague /: *around Anno 1657* :/ and since that time she has not seen the boy, therefore she could not know if he was still alive.

4. *Whether, while he was playing one time with the son of the Commander, she didn't grab the same by the head and spin him around,*

Says, yes, she did that. The children had been hitting each other, they were throwing sand into each other's eyes, she didn't do the boy any harm with that.

5. *Whether the boy didn't fall to the ground,*
Says, yes.

6. *Whether he didn't call her an old whore,*
Says, yes, he did that.

7. *Whether thereupon she didn't wave with her hand saying, "You'll regret that, before three days are over,"*
Says, yes, that was no severed neck.[1] The child walked away, no harm came to him. Next time she won't warn children any more, they can fall into the fire or the water.

8. *Whether upon the 4th day one of the herder's cattle didn't take ill and die,*
Says yes, the cattle got or caught the blood.[2]

9. *Whether 14 days afterwards one of the cows of the same didn't take ill and fall over in the heather,*
Says she doesn't know anything about that, it happens often.

10. *Whether 4 weeks later one of the herder's pigs didn't fall ill and die,*
Says yes, it caught a *Muller* out of the earth, that is, a groundhog, and ate it.

11. *Whether it isn't true that no one else's cattle died,*
Says, she didn't know that, she has forgotten that. If it had happened a few years ago, eight years is too long a time.

12. *Whether when the herder moved away 6 years ago one more cow didn't take ill on the way and die in Beienrode,*
Says, she doesn't know that, should she lose her head for that?[3]

---

1 A matter of life and death.
2 This refers to bloody diarrhea, usually dysentery.
3 Literally, "whether for that her neck should be sneezed off."

13. *Whether the imprisoned didn't do all that to the cattle, that they died, and how and by what means did she do it,*
Says, no, why should she, she isn't crazy, and she wishes her neighbours well, just as herself.

14. *Whether in the end she didn't bewitch the aforementioned son of the herder, so that his left leg swelled up very thickly,*
Says, no, instead the boy jumped across the water in front of his father's, Hans Wolter's, door, with that he sprained his leg, she saw that just when she wanted to go to the garden to get cabbage.

15. *Whether she didn't come to the sick child's house and gave the same a yellow pear,*
Says, yes, she brought the same two pears, more specifically two knight's pears.[1]

16. *Whether she didn't put the pear on the mantle in a pot, because the sick boy wouldn't accept it,*
Says yes, she put the two pears in the mentioned place.

17. *What did she put into this pear that made the inside look all black,*
Says, she put nothing in it, the pear must have been mealy, soft or doughy, so that it looked black, also it had black seeds.

18. *Whether she didn't prepare the pear through witchcraft in such a way that the sick boy got severe pains from it low in his body,*
Says, no, the almighty God shall save her from that, they have to prove that.

19. *Whether she didn't make it so that the lower body swelled from this pear,*
Says, no.

20. *Whether a messenger wasn't sent to her to help the boy,*
Says, yes, the boy's mother came to her herself, but she, the imprisoned, answered the same that she could not help the child.

---

1   This is an old variety of pear that is now no longer available.

2 1 . *Whether she didn't come and say "Be quiet, you won't die from this,"*
Says, yes, she said that.

2 2 . *Whether Inquisitin didn't give the witness's husband to understand that he should carry the sick child to the garden onto the turned soil behind the house,*
Says, yes, she said that.

2 3 . *Whether on Inquisitin's instructions he didn't have to lie on his back and stretch his hands and feet,*
Says, yes, she gave those instructions.

2 4 . *Whether she didn't step up and plant something by the child's hands and feet and also by the head, what was it and what was it for,*
Says, yes, she did that, and it was linseed, was supposed to help the child, who was afflicted in the hands and feet, and complained loudly about pain, because linseed or flax does not grow or sprout more than the length of a finger, and then it goes away again and is gone, now as the flax goes away again, in the same way the pain goes away, and when the flax is planted like that, you have to walk around it three times. But nothing is said during this, while doing it you can say anything you like. She once had a book in which this is written, but the book has gone missing.

2 5 . *Whether the swineherd of Bechtsbüttel didn't find her sitting by the fire one evening when he came home,*
Says, she doesn't know that.

2 6 . *Whether he didn't start in at her "How is it, will you help him up, or will you let him lie,"*
Says, she doesn't know that.

2 7 . *Whether he didn't grab the battle axe from the wall and wanted to strike Inquisitin with it,*
Says, yes, he said he wanted to cut off her old neck, she replied and said, "Yes, cut it off," and there was loud quarreling, because the swineherd had had a bit to drink.

2 8 . *Whether she didn't jump away then, and stayed away from Harxbüttel a whole 9 weeks,*

Says, yes, she said, "Don't be crazy," thereupon she hurried out of the house walking or running to the door, and because she was fetched to Bortfeld to a sick man, named Heinrich Rehke, who was so ailing, and is now all dead, so she stayed five weeks in Bortfeld, during which time she didn't come to Harxbüttel.

29. *Whether half a year ago a woman from Essenrode didn't come to her,*
Says, no.

30. *Whether the same woman didn't ask Inquisitin for advice, how she could get the former toll collector in marriage,*
Says, no, the Devil may take her if such a loose woman had been with her or if she had given her advice.

31. *Whether she didn't give her something that she was to administer to the toll collector, what was it, and what effect should it have had on him, also how did it turn out?*
Cessat.

32. *Whether 9 years ago in Neubrück she didn't get completely drunk with Stoffel Jürgens at master Heinrich Cordes's, as in act. N. 20,*
Says, no honest person should say that about her, but by this she did not mean the interrogators. While she remembers that some years ago in Wenden in Heinrich Cordes's house with the same and Stoffel Jürgens, each drank a half *Stübchen* of beer.

33. *Whether at the same time she didn't come to Heinrich Cordes's bed, as in N. 20,*
Says, yes.

34. *Whether she didn't say there was a mandrake in his house that wanted to move away,*
Says, well yes, she did say that.

35. *Whether she didn't demand half a Taler, to make it so that it had to stay,*
Says, yes, but she got nothing and it was only a joke or teasing.

36. *Whether she didn't that same day bewitch the five year old child of Heinrich Cordes,*

Says, oh no, not that, the child had worms, there are such strange people in the world, when a fly walks on their body, it must be called witchcraft. One always wants to cross the fence where it is lowest.

37. *Whether she didn't bring it about through witch's art, that a black thing appeared to the child, that wanted to get the child,*
Says, oh no, not that, oh not that, surely a child can imagine something.

38. *What kind of thing it was, and whether it wasn't her lover the Evil Enemy,*
Says, she didn't know that, she didn't know the Devil, Jesus Christ may preserve us from that, surely they would not talk her neck away /: *talk so much that it might cost her her neck* :/ our Lord God would give counsel.

39. *Whether Cordes didn't threaten her through Stoffel Jürgens that she should take this away from the child again, or he will have her dealt with another way,*
Says, yes, he had her threatened, but she had done nothing to the child.

40. *Whether upon hearing these threatening words she didn't remove it from the child again and said through Stoffel Jürgens: "Stoffel, there is nothing wrong with the boy,"*
Says, yes, because nothing was wrong with the child, except that he had worms. *Addit.*[1] She can now see that people were out to get her, the *Inquisitin.*

41. *Whether she didn't promise the miller, Christoff Meinicke, that he would get so many customers that they would fight each other for his milling,*
Says, the miller talked to her about that, she gave him a piece of baptized cowl or dress, the same small skin that some children bring into the world with them at birth and don't need, the miller was to carry that on his person in order to get many milling clients. For that the miller gave her a dried eel and a home-baked bread. It happened one time that a soldier's whore gave birth in the open field, and because nobody wanted to look after her, she went to her and helped the woman. When the child entered the world it had such a small extra skin or dress. *Inquisitin* pulled that off the child when she bathed it and later had the skin baptized with

---

1   "Additional comment."

the child in Wenden, as she put the same with the child in the diaper, and she kept it afterwards.

42. *Whether she didn't give him several dried roots for that, what kind of roots they were, and from whom she got the same,*
Says, yes, she gave him the roots, like carline thistle and angelica, she bought them here in Brunswick in the big apothecary for 1*g*.

43. *Whether she didn't order him to sew the roots in his clothes and to keep them warm,*
Says, yes.

44. *Whether she didn't say to the miller's helper that he had made a woman pregnant, who will bring him the child some day soon,*
Says, no, but other people said that.

45. *How did she know that, whether it wasn't her lover the Evil Enemy who revealed it to her,*
Says, as *ad proxe praecedentem Articulum Inquistionalem.*

46. *Whether she added that the woman liked to get drunk and was Catholic,*
Cessat.

47. *Whether she didn't help Christoff Rieckmann of Thune as well as his wife and children with a serious illness. What kind of illness was it, and how did she cure the same, what did she use for it and who taught her,*
Says, yes.
And those people were lame in hands and feet, she bound green chervil on their hands, which she had first pounded or mashed. And gave them *Heilebarts* /: stork's :/ dung, at the same time she gave them angelica root, that had a strong good smell, and *Heilbartsklapper*[1] that grow so on the water, as well as *Allard Schwerdtai* roots and green *Ballei* after the speci-fied had beforehand been boiled down to half in a quart of beer, from which they had to drink. Likewise she took three *Spiegel*[2] of *Pagelun* or

---

1   *Heilbart* is a local name for a stork and *Klapper* means "rattle". So the name is "stork's rattle." Possibly it is yellow iris, *iris pseudacorus*. The next two, *Allard Schwerdtai* and *Ballei*, we could not identify.

2   Literally, "mirror." This may refer to the round, shiny centres of a peacock feather.

peacock feathers cut small, and because otherwise they are hard to swallow because they always swim at the top, she baked the cut feathers in an egg, so that the patients could take the feathers in this way, because the people were without sense in their head, and the peacock feathers are supposed to help with that, and this art she learned in a book, she wishes that she still had it, as she had lost it, because she loaned it out so often.

48. *Whether she didn't say that the person who had given them the illness should soon come to Riekmann's house to borrow something,*
Says, no, she didn't do that, even if she should be hung or roasted!

49. *Whether she didn't do sorcery to the said person so that the person had to come there, how she had done that, and who had taught her,*
Cessat.

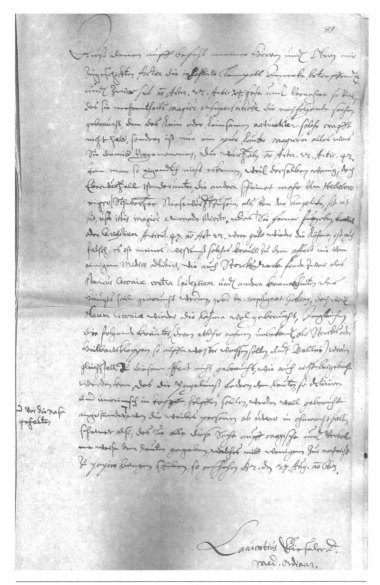

Figure 5 First page of Folio 23: The medical judgment of Laurentius Gieseler. This judgment by the *Stadtphysicus* concerned Tempel Anneke's use of herbs described in Folio 22. It is written and signed in his own hand.

Folio 23

[In her answer to questions 24, 42, and 47 of Folio 21, Tempel Anneke described a number of herbs that she used in her cures. In this document the Stadtphysicus testifies that these herbs could not work naturally in the way she claims.]

Herr Doctoris Gieseler Medici judaeum.[1]

From the documents sent to me on the order of my masters and superiors concerning the imprisoned Tempel Anneke, specifically *sub no. Acten.* 22. *Artic.* 24. I see and become aware of this much that she frequently used the following things *magice et superstitiose.*[2] Since flax or linseed does not have such power *naturaliter,*[3] but it is all pure *magicum,*[4] all that she did with it. The roots in *Acten* 22. *Artic.* 42, one cannot recognize because they are rare, but carline thistle is among them, the other seems more to be *Helleboro nigro* /: Christmas Rose[5] :/ than angelica. *Sit ut non sit usa istis magice et modo illicito.*[6] What she asserted further, *Articul.* 47. *No. Act.* 22., that chervil or *cerefolium* is supposed to be good against lameness, is also wrong. According to my knowledge such an herb is never used to such an effect by any *medico.*[7] As with stork dung, while I find that *Stercus Ciconia*[8] is said to be used *contra Epilepsiam*[9] and other illnesses of the head, *quod Dn. Impugnat Galeny,*[10] it is *oleum Ciconia*[11] that is often used against lameness. The following herbs (of which several names are unknown, like stork's- or *Heilbarts*-rattle[12] that are supposed to grow on water, and *Ballei*) similarly are also not used for this effect. Although it cannot be taught that peacock feathers should help people

---

1   "Medical judgment of Doctor Gieseler."
2   "Magically and superstitiously."
3   "Naturally."
4   "Magic."
5   See the illustration of Christmas Rose on p. 162.
6   "In any case, she uses them in a magical and illicit way."
7   Doctor.
8   Stork dung.
9   Against epilepsy.
10 "Whereas in opposition to Dr. Galen…"
11 Stork oil.
12 See n. 1, p. 77.

who are delirious and nonsensical in the head, they are often used lit and held under the nose, when women faint *ab utero*.[1] Therefore it appears that she gave all these things to the people in magical and forbidden ways. This was to be put to paper concisely, as was done.

Brunswick, the 27th of August *Anno* 1663

Laurentius Gieseler

D. med. ordinar.

---

[1] "From the uterus."

Folio 24

[Following the questioning of Tempel Anneke on August 24, the trial records were sent to the legal faculty of the University of Jena for an opinion
on the evidence against the accused. On the basis of this judgment the court
had the legal authority on which to proceed to torture.]

To the noble, honourable and well-learned, most and very wise mayors and
councillors of the city of Brunswick, our gracious gentlemen and friends.

First our willing offering of service! Knightly, most well-learned, high
and very wise, gracious gentlemen and friends! As the same have sent us
the documents of the investigation against the imprisoned Anna Roleffes,
otherwise called Tempel Anneke, and desired our legal advice concerning
the same, we rightfully pronounce after careful reading and consideration
of the same:

That the said *Inquisitin* should be questioned again concerning the denied
inquisitional articles found in the documents, without torture and in the presence of the executioner and his torture instruments, and, if she does not
confess right away, because of the strong evidence against the same, to question her with torture, and with appropriate pressure, and to carefully record
her testimony, whereupon what is right will come about.

Officially certified by law with our seal.
Ordinarius, Decanus, Senior[1] and other doctors of the Faculty of Law at the
University of Jena.

---

1   These are ranks of the doctors of law at the University of Jena.

Folio 25

[On the basis of the legal decision from Jena, the Higher Court here identi-
fies a list of questions from Folios 2 and 21 on which to re-examine Tempel
Anneke under threat of torture and under torture if necessary.]

Articuli sub num. Ad. 2 and 21,
which the imprisoned previously denied, and because of that shall be examined in other ways about it *in praesentia carnificis*,[1] and {...} with torture,
through the power of the legal decision obtained.[2]

Extract
of the *inquisitional articul sub num act.* 2.
denied by *Inquisitin* Anna Roleffes on the 1st of July.
Numbers 10. 11. 13. 14. 15. 16. 21. 23. 24. 25. 26. 37. 38. 41. 44. 45. 46.
47. 48. 49. 50. 53. 55. 57. 58. 59. 60. 61. and 62.

Extract
Articul. Inquisitinal sub num. act. 21.
Numbers 9. 11. 12. 13. 14. 17. 18. 19. 29. 30. 31. 32. 36. 37. 38. 39. 44.
45. 48. and 49.

---

1   "In the presence of the executioner."
2   The decision referred to is the *Gutachten* received from the University of Jena, in Folio 24. See
    p. xxxiii of the Introduction.

Folio 26

[In this folio are Tempel Anneke's answers under the threat of torture to the questions identified in Folio 25.]

The specific content of the *Articulos*, previously denied by *Inquisitin* Anna Roleffes, otherwise called Tempel Anneke, now again her answers given without torture and with accompanying *Territion*.[1]

The 21st and 22nd *Octobris Anno* 1663

Actum in the municipal jail of Hagen
The 21st *Octobris Anno* 1663

By the honourable Gabriel Oeding and the honourable Henning Blome, both officers of the court, then Johann Velhagen and Otto Theune, both magistrates of the court and Johann Pilgram, the court scribe.

Through the power of the legal decision obtained, *Inquisitin* Anna Roleffes, otherwise known as Tempel Anneke, is questioned, first concerning the *Inquisitionalis Artos*, composed in the *sub. Num. Act.* 2. and then denied in *Num* 3. of the *Actis* of the 1st of July, in the manner laid out here, again without torture, and specifically according to the findings and the necessity of the matter, with the introduction of the executioner, and with the showing of the instruments belonging to torture, and what she answered to each, registered with all possible care, and described *formalibus verbis*.

Num. Act. 2.

Ad.

10. *Whether she didn't promise him [Tiehmann] that she would be able to frighten the thief who stole what belonged to him, so that before 24 hours had passed, he should have his things back,*

---

1   This term refers to the showing of the torture instruments to the accused, although "showing" involves demonstration, and so it is really the beginning of torture.

Says, yes, she promised Tiehmann to torture the thief in such a way, that
Tiehmann should get back what belonged to him, in which way he also
did get back what was his. But that this was to occur within 24 hours,
she didn't say. She also didn't say "frighten," but that she would torture
the thief, and torture is as much as frighten.

11. *Whether she asked him to come back to her on the 3rd day after,*
Says, she said to Tiehmann he should come back to her in three or four
days.

13. *Whether she didn't frighten the thief as she had promised so that he brought back
some of the stolen things of Tiehmann's,*
Says, yes,

14. *How and in which way did she do it,*
Says, she took a piece of a man's shirt, and wound the same around a
plug /: *taken from a beer barrel* :/ at her son's house in Harxbüttel, and
shoved it into a hole in a support post in the barn, which was drilled
into it by the carpenters at the time when the barn was raised, like they
bored many similar holes. And she said these words while hitting it in,
"You thief, if you stole what belonged to the fellow, then you should
return that to him within a few days, or your heart will burst in your
body." She didn't say more while doing it, and also she didn't hit more
than three times with a large stone, and such a hole must not be bored
through to the back, and also no air must get in, because as long as a
hole like that is closed, stays plugged, a thief because of whom it was
hammered in cannot have air to the heart.

Asked whether, while hitting or hammering three times with the stone, she
didn't use any words,
Says, no, no more words than she already said, but also while she was hitting three times she spoke, "in the name of the Father, Son and Holy Spirit."

15. *Whether she didn't plug the thief into a drilled hole in the name of the Evil
Enemy, so that the fellow squeaked inside it like a heap of mice,*
Says consistently, no.

Hereupon the executioner is presented to her, and the same started to show the instruments belonging to torture, but *Inquisitin* stood consistently by her denials, and burst out angrily, and said: by the sacrament, what is she supposed to say, because she has nothing to do with the Devil.

But also now as *Inquisitin* was talked to by the executioner, she finally confessed and admitted, that she plugged the hole as described above in the name of the Devil /: *God protect us* :/ that the man's heart in his body was supposed to squeak like a heap of mice, that's how much it was supposed to hurt him.

16. *How did she know how the fellow, who stole from Tiehmann, fed himself, and how many children he had,*
    Says, how Tiehman, three or four days later, came to her again, and reported to her, that he had got his things back, except for a tin bowl, which he had not yet got. Thereupon she hit the plug loose again, pulled the same out with the linen cloth, and threw both together in the name of the Devil onto the hearth into the fire in her son's house, while she said, "Lie there and burn in the name of the Devil." How she then saw that three sparks flew out of the fire, one after the other, and she could notice from that that the thief had to be a poor man, and she informed Tiehmann of this, who was sitting in the pub, and had sent word to her. In fact, she didn't know the man, also couldn't know him, only as she threw the plug into the fire, she saw from the sparks that it must be a poor man, and one spark meant the man himself, but the other two sparks meant two children.

21. *Whether, because he would not let her have any [more beer], she didn't conjure an injury into his [Hans Harves's] thigh,*
    Says, no.

Inquisitin was advised that Hans Harves had strengthed this with his oath, whereupon she answered that he gave his oath like a rogue. He can take responsibility for that.

The executioner showed her another instrument, put the same on the feet of *Inquisitin*, reminded her to speak the truth. *Inquisitin* stood consistently by her denial, saying, Hans Harves should have learned his Ten Commandments.

23. *Whether Hennig Vaddrian on the Knochenhauer Street in Hagen didn't once come to her because of an injury like that,*
Says, no.

Even though she was now seriously talked to, in spite of this she stood consistently by her denial.

24. *Whether Harves didn't let her be told through the same, that he got his ailment from no one else but her,*
Cessat.

25. *Whether she wasn't threatened, if she wouldn't remove the injury from him, that he would look for help in another place,*
Cessat.

26. *Whether he didn't add that, if she were innocent, she should come and deny the charge,*
Cessat.

37. *From whom did she learn this [to heal the cattle], and whether this didn't happen through sorcery,*
Says, from a cavalry boy of the Emperor's people, about 20 years ago, he was billeted at her house with cavalrymen. But when she was talked to seriously she referred to a woman from Wittenberg, who came to this region about 20 years ago and stayed at her son's house for four weeks as a lodger, and she made something for the people but she died several years later in Walle. She gave her lessons, how she had to do the plugging. The young soldier boy did it in the same way. Because the horses were stolen from the stable at night, he plugged a piece of a shirt in this way, and they got the horses back. Whether that was sorcery she didn't know, if it were sorcery then she would be in for it.

38. *Whether she didn't conjure something into the left arm of Hans Harves's house wife, that extended to the left hand and made the hand swell thickly,*
Says consistently, no. That can't be said, sending it into the arms, sending it into the legs. God would punish Harves and his wife that they said that on the neck of *Inquisitin*.

The executioner did his reminding, *Inquistin* stood by her denial.

41. *Whether she didn't order Lüdecke Tau's wife to bring the head of a dead cow from Bortfeld into the house of Inquisitin,*
Says, yes.

42. *What did she do with it, and what did she need it for,*
Says, she didn't need the head, instead she threw the same in the water,

43. *Whether she didn't throw the head into the water so that when Hans Harves rowed over the spot, he should get the injury to the leg,*
Says, yes, but the head stank so much that she could not brew it to powder, that's why she threw it into the water, not so that Hans Harves should be harmed by it.

44. *Whether she didn't offer to help them when dying befell the sheep in Harxbüttel,*
Says, she didn't offer that, rather the *Schafmeisterse*,[1] the widow of Hans Davidt, was then at her son's house in Harxbüttel, and she still stays there, talked to her about it. *Inquisitin* got these herbs for the same from the field: angelica root, field hops, lungwort, wild sage, meadow blackberry or wormwood and wood hops, and the sheep master's wife cooked them together, and with the powder of the dead sheep, that the *Schafmeisterse* took from the fallen animals, and fried in the oven to a powder, administered it three times, and with that the dying of the animals slowed.

45. *Whether she didn't bring the sickness through sorcery amongst the sheep,*
Says, no.

The executioner presented himself, urged *Inquisitin*, showed her more *instrumenta*,[2] but *Inquisitin* stood by her denial.

46. *How, and by which means did she want to help the sheep,*

---

1 The feminine form of "sheep master."
2 "Instruments."

Says, she couldn't help the sheep, and repeats what she answered today ad 44.

47. *Whether she didn't burn a sheep from the herd to powder in the oven, cooked something in a kettle, and administered it to the sheep,*
Says, that the *Schafmeisterse* burned the sheep to powder herself according to *Inquisitin's* instructions. And she, *Inquisitin,* as previously reported fetched the herbs for that from the field, because *Inquisitin* saw from a sheep master in the Niendorff monastery near Gardelegen, how he burned the sheep in this way to powder, and administered something of that to the others, so that they shouldn't die away in droves.

48. *Whether she didn't learn such things from the Evil Enemy,*
Says, no, she learned and saw that from the sheep master at the Niendorff monastery.

49. *Whether she didn't conjure something into the left leg of Hennig Roleffes of Wenden, so that it broke open,*
Says consistently, no. Hennig *LeygenRumpff* /: liar :/ could say what he wants.

The executioner did his reminding to speak the truth, *Inquisitin* stood by her denial.

50. *Whether whenever he caught sight of her his whole body swelled thickly, and this happened four times,*
Says, she knew nothing about that, she is innocent of that.

53. *Whether at the wedding of the sheep master of Harxbüttel she didn't say to the wife of Hans Vette, that she could lock and unlock and that Hennig Roleffes must still do better,*
Says consistently, no.

Even though she was herewith greatly urged, she still did not want to waver from her denials, and she apologized that in truth she does not know what to say differently.

55. *Whether she didn't conjure the evil things into the head of Jürgen Roleffes, so that he turned completely dense from it,*
Says, she didn't do that, Jürgen Roleffes got that in the head from our Lord God, not from her.

The *Inquisitin* was talked to, the executioner was presented to her, who took his other *instrumenta* in hand, yet *Inquisitin* stood by her denial.

57. *Whether six years ago she didn't inform Autor Bahrensdorff where his horse and foals could be found, which he believed to be lost,*
Says, she said he should look for the horses in front of the woods, because in fairness she had pointed towards the high gate, she didn't know the name of the woods.

58. *Where did she know it from,*
Says, she knew nothing about it, only that she had said that he should go to the woods. That the horses were found there she didn't know beforehand, that was no sorcery.

Even though the executioner made to *Inquisitin* as if he wanted to attack her, in spite of that she stood consistently by her denial, that she had not divined it.

59. *Whether at that time she didn't want to help two sick children of Lüdecke Thies the wheel maker here, and how did that go,*
Says, the children had dropsy, that was situated between skin and flesh and that is called dropsy and it is caused by drinking a lot. She cooked fresh flax for the children, and gave them the water from that, yet that didn't want to help them, that was too slow, their hands and feet had already become inflamed or swollen.

60. *Whether she didn't use such forbidden arts more, where, on whom, how, and how long,*
Says, she helped others, like a child in Eichhorst, his age was 4 years, whose father was a school master and was called Ludvcke Schaper, and moved from Eichhorst to Lütken Jesen. For this child she brewed rue, wormwood and roasted salt, and that was administered to the children three or four times. In addition she also helped the old and the young,

who had problems with their *Hachtmutter*, these she gave something from the *Hachtmutter* from *quappen Fehe.*[1]

61. *Whether she didn't make a pact with the Evil Enemy, and through his help committed such deeds,*
Says consistently, no. Threw out her hands, saying she made no pact with the Devil, she had nothing to do with the Devil.

Hereupon it is pointed out to her that nevertheless she hammered in the plug in the name of the Devil. To that she answered, how does that happen, to plug something in such a name, and to have a pact with him. She has nothing to do with the Devil, come what may.

Master Hans, the executioner, also urged *Inquisitin*, but she would not comment in any other way.

62. *How and in which form did he come to her, how did she join together with him, Cessat.*

Continuatio[2]

Actum in the municipal jail of Hagen
the 22nd 8bris *Anno* 1663

By all of the persons of the court mentioned at the beginning

Through the power of the legal decision obtained, *Inquisitin* was further questioned without torture, and particularly *in praesentia* of the executioner, concerning the following specified questions composed in *Actis. Num.* 21. and then denied the 24th of August *Num.* 22, and her testimony thereto was described *formalibus verbis.*[3]

Ad.
9. *Whether 14 days afterwards one of the cows of the same [Hans Wolter] didn't take ill and fall over in the heather,*

---

1 The words *Hachtmutter* and *quappen Fehe* are transcribed as they appear in the document, but we could not find translations for them.
2 "Continuation."
3 "Using the proper words."

Says, she has no knowledge of that, started to cry and said, that would move God in heaven to pity, that she should say what she did not know.

11. *Whether it isn't true that no one else's cattle died,*
Says, she didn't know that.

12. *Whether when the herder moved away 6 years ago one more cow didn't take ill on the way and die in Beienrode,*
Says, she really didn't know that, could not add anything to that.

13. *Whether the imprisoned didn't do all that to the cattle, that they died, and how and by what means did she do it,*
Says, no, what advantage would she have got from the man's damage, she didn't do it, she hit her chest and said, she was willing to answer to God that she didn't do it.

14. *Whether finally she didn't bewitch the aforementioned son of the herder, so that his left leg swelled up very thickly,*
Says consistently, no.

Even though she was urged at this point, the executioner also confronted her, and reminded her to speak the truth, she still stood consistently by her denial.

17. *What did she put into the pear that made the inside look all black,*
Says, she didn't put anything into it, it must have been black from the pit.

18. *Whether she didn't prepare the pear through witchcraft in such a way that the sick boy got severe pains from it low in his body,*
Says, she didn't do that. No, no.

19. *Whether she didn't make it so the lower body swelled from this pear,*
Says, she didn't do that, she gave the pear to the child with the best intentions.

29. *Whether half a year ago a woman from Essenrode didn't come to her,*
No, no, no. She knows no one in Essenrode.

30. *Whether the same woman didn't ask Inquisitin for advice, how she could get the former toll collector in marriage,*
Says consistently, no, God have mercy.

31. *Whether she didn't give her something that she was to administer to the toll collector, what was it, and what effect should it have on him, also how did it turn out,*
Says, she didn't do that.

During the aforementioned questioning the executioner did his reminding *in specie*,[1] and carefully urged *Inquisitin*, but she did not answer any more, other than saying, "No, no Master Hans."

32. *Whether 9 years ago in Neubrück she didn't get completely drunk with Stoffel Jürgens at master Heinrich Cordes's,*
Says, that was and happened in Wenden, at Heinrich Cordes's house.

36. *Whether she didn't that same day bewitch the five year old child of Heinrich Cordes,*
Says, she didn't do that. Instead she said the child had worms in him, they should give the same saffron seed and chalk in sweet milk.

37. *Whether she didn't bring it about through witches's art, that a black thing appeared to the child, which wanted to get the child,*
Says, she didn't do that.

38. *What kind of thing it was, and whether it wasn't her lover the Evil Enemy, Cessat.*

39. *Whether Cordes didn't threaten her through Stoffel Jürgens that she should take this away from the child again, or he will have her dealt with another way,*
Says, yes, he threatened her, only she hadn't done the child any harm, but the same had a swollen body because of many worms.

44. *Whether she didn't say to the miller's helper that he had made a woman pregnant, who will bring him the child some day soon,*

---

1 "In appearance or pretence."

Says, no, what should she know about the maid, the miller's wife had said to *Inquisitin* that a Catholic woman wanted to bring their helper a child.

45. *How she did know that, whether it wasn't her lover the Evil Enemy who revealed it to her,*
Cessat.

48. *Whether she didn't say that the person who had given them [Christoff Riekmann of Thune as well as his wife and children] the illness should soon come to Riekmann's house to borrow something,*
Says, that wasn't so.

With this the executioner, as happened with the previous *Articulis*, did his serious reminder, only *Inquisitin* in spite of that stood by her denial.

49. *Whether she didn't do sorcery to the said person [who had given them the illness], so that the person had to come there, how she did that, and who taught her,*
Cessat.

Folio 27

[The court here formulates a set of questions about which to interrogate Tempel Anneke under torture.]

Extracted *Articuli* denied by the prisoner, Anna Roleffes, during previous *Territion*, concerning which the same shall be examined with real torture or sharp questioning.

Articuli about which *Captiva* shall be interrogated during the application of torture,

1. Where did she learn that she could see from the sparks of fire a man's poverty, and the number of his children,

2. Whether she didn't conjure an injury into the thigh of Hans Harves of Harxbüttel, because one day he didn't want to have beer sent to her,

3. How she brought this about,

4. Whether Hennig Vaddrian, of Knochenhauer Street in Hagen, once came to her because of such an injury,

5. Whether Harves didn't let her be told through the same that he had his injury from nobody but her,

6. Whether Harves didn't threaten her, that if she would not take his injury away, he wanted to look elsewhere,

7. Whether he didn't add, that if she were innocent, she should come and answer the charge,

8. From whom had she learned her arts and especially the sorcery,

9. Whether she didn't conjure something into the left arm of Hans Harves's wife,

10. Whether she didn't throw the head of a dead animal in the water near Harxbüttel to the end that when Hans Harves rowed across it his leg would be damaged,

11. Whether she didn't bring death among the sheep through sorcery,

12. Whether she didn't learn from the Evil Enemy that one is supposed to burn sheep to powder and to give that to the sheep to prevent them from dying,

13. Whether she didn't conjure something into the left leg of Hennig Roleffes of Wenden,

14. Whether she didn't say to the wife of Hans Vette, at the wedding of the sheep master, that she could lock and unlock and whether that doesn't happen through sorcery,

15. Whether she didn't conjure the evil things into Jürgen Roleffes's head, that he turned totally dense from that,

16. How did she do that, and from where did she get the evil things,

17. Whether six years ago she didn't let Autor Bahrensdorff know where his lost horses and foals were,

18. How did she know that,

19. Whether she didn't make a pact with the Evil Enemy, and accomplish the aforesaid deeds through his help,

20. How and in what form did the same come to her,

21. Whether she didn't do damage to people and animals, or else fruits of the field,

22. How did she accomplish it every time, and whether the Evil Spirit directed her and taught her,

23. Whether she fornicated with the same in unnatural ways, how often, and in which place,

24. Whether she accomplished the evil things through these means,

25. Whether she didn't bewitch the animals of Hans Wolter, the current swineherd in Bechtsbüttel, while the same still stayed in Harxbüttel, so that they died,

26. Whether she didn't bewitch the left leg of the son of the same swineherd,

27. Whether she didn't give a pear, prepared through witchcraft, to the swineherd's son, and to what end did she do this,

28. Whether she didn't bewitch Heinrich Cordes's child,

29. Whether she didn't bring it about through witches's arts that a black thing appeared to the child that wanted to get the child.

Folio 28

[In this folio Tempel Anneke answers the questions in Folio 27 under the first full application of torture. Here she confesses fully to the crime of witchcraft.]

The confession made by *Inquisitin* Anna Roleffes, otherwise called Tempel Anneke, following the application of torture, on the extracted *Inquisitional Articul* formulated in *Act. Num.* 27, and what she said in addition voluntarily.

The 22nd October *Anno* 1663

Actum in Brunswick in Hagen in the deep cellar

By all the appointed officers of the court and the court magistrates of the city of Brunswick, municipality of Hagen.

Because *Inquisitin* Anna Roleffes, otherwise called Tempel Anneke, concealed the truth on various *Inquisitionales* during the previous *Territion*, so she is taken today at seven in the evening, into the deep cellar, and further interrogated about the extracted *Inquisitionales* formulated in *Actis Num.* 27, and what she answered to each of them *formalibus verbis*, was carefully recorded, and according to all of which she testified:

Ad.

1. *Where did she learn that she could see from the sparks of fire a man's poverty, and the number of his children,*

   Says, from the woman from Wittenberg, named Catharina N., because the same told her, if there are small sparks, they are children, but big sparks, that is a woman and a man, now because there had been two small sparks, that meant the children, but two big sparks meant a woman and a man /: *the thief and his wife* :/ because when she threw the plug into the fire, four sparks flew out of the fire.

   Because, of the 4 previously mentioned sparks, the one spark was black—that means it didn't burn as brightly as the others—from that she was able to see, according to the teachings of the woman from Wittenberg, that it was a poor man who committed the theft.

[98]

Asked why she testified today that only three sparks flew up when she threw the plug into the fire, why she is now testifying that it had been 4 sparks, and what they had meant. Says, she didn't remember today, as she does now, she got confused, questioned back and forth.

Hereupon the executioner blindfolded *Inquisitin*, put the ligature[1] on her, also he put a leg screw on her left leg, but because she declared that she would like to say the pure truth, the leg screw was loosened, and she was further questioned *ad*:

2. *Whether she didn't conjure an injury into the thigh of Hans Harves of Harxbüttel, because one day he didn't want to have beer sent to her,*
   Says, she didn't do that, they should let her have time to answer.

3. *How she brought this about,*
   Cessat.

4. *Whether Hennig Vaddrian, of Knochenhauer Street in Hagen, once came to her because of such an injury,*
   Says, Vaddrian did indeed come there, and he wanted to buy rams from the shepherd, only he didn't talk to her, as stated before.

5. *Whether Harves didn't let her be told through the same that he had his injury from nobody but her,*
   Says, Vaddrian said nothing to her face that she had heard. But she asked the shoe mender /: *who lived on Inquisitin's son's farm* :/, he didn't want to tell her what Vaddrian had said. The shoe mender only said that she should come to the Tempel /: *to the pub* :/ but she didn't go.

6. *Whether Harves didn't threaten her, that if she would not take his injury away, he wanted to look elsewhere,*
   Says, he might have done that, but she didn't hear it from him.

7. *Whether he didn't add, that if she were innocent, she should come and answer the charge,*
   Says, she didn't hear that.

---

1   This is a leather binding around the head. It was commonly used together with the leg screw.

8. *From whom did she learn her arts and especially the sorcery,*
   Says, from a woman from Wittenberg.

But as the executioner, following this, tightened the leg screw again, and talked seriously to her, she declared again that she would speak the truth, and after the leg screw was loosened she confessed that she learned the sorcery half a score years ago /: *that is, 10 years ago* :/ from the *Martensche* of Wenden—already taken by death—because her brother Hennig Roleffes,[1] who at that time lived on the Tempel Hof, had two sick cows, and one turned completely lame. Because of them, *Inquisitin* went to aforementioned *Martensche* of Wenden, and asked the same for advice, because the same was able to help people in that way. She had given advice to *Inquisitin* and said she wanted to send *Inquisitin* a man, who was supposed to bring herbs to *Inquisitin*. At night when she was still awake but soon wanted to go lie /: *that is, to bed* :/ the black man came to the door, and knocked pik, pik, pik. When she went outside and asked, who is there, and what kind of man he was, he said, "Behold, there you have herbs, give that to the cows, the woman you went to see had me do this." And after she took the herbs, she saw the man no more, but the herbs she gave to the cows. About three days later, the black man came back to her at night, came in front of her bed and said to her, "Listen you, what I tell you, you are supposed to do. If you have an enemy, I will fly there." When she then said Hans Köhler of Vollbüttel five or six years ago now had called her a terrible whore and a cunt, because of that she wanted, when he drove across the meadow, to seize the horse and take the reins.[2] The black man answered, did she want to put up with that, he would not do that, she should order him and say, "Fly there, you should handle him, as much as I want." When then *Inquisitin* said she didn't really want to murder the man, the black man answered, he wanted to fly into the man's leg. And from that time on the man's left leg withered, even though it didn't cause any pain, even less did he die of it, rather he is still alive.

Several days after that the black man came to her again, and because a man called Til Schwartz from Leiferde of Papenteich[3] had run her down, she directed him that he must kill the horse with which she had been run down.

---

1 This is a different person from Hennig Roleffes of Wenden.
2 This implies a legal seizure, which could be done by a civilian under local custom when animals were in a field to which their owner had no rights.
3 Papenteich is a wood north of Harxbüttel. See *Im Papendicke* on Map 3, p. xxii.

It was a brown horse. About 2 years ago the man had fallen into a millpole[1] but didn't die from that. She didn't do any more than that, she had also made no pact with *Satanas /: as her formalia said*[2] *:/* or promised him anything, his name was Til Kleppersack.[3]

> 9. *Whether she didn't conjure something into the left arm of Hans Harves's wife,*
> Says consistently, no.

> 10. *Whether she didn't throw the head of a dead cow in the water near Harxbüttel to the end that when Hans Harves rowed across it his leg would be damaged,*
> Says, he didn't get it from the head.
>
> Asked: *what then did he get it from instead?*
> Says, she didn't know that.

But as the executioner used the other screw, on the left leg of *Inquisitin*, she confessed after the loosening of that one and the other screw, that a woman called Catharina, widow Böschke, at that time housewife in Walle, buried a pot under an *Alhorn /: elderberry :/* bush, *Inquisitin* didn't know what was in it, in order that *Inquisitin*'s brother Heinrich Roleffes, who later went to war, would walk over it and should get and become like Hans Harves of the Tempel had become, that is to say, what befell Hans Harves should befall her brother, because her brother had slept with the daughter of the mentioned Catharina. And when he was supposed to marry her, he went away to war, because of that Catharina was so angry with him. But she, *Inquisitin*, wasn't responsible for that, but rather became aware of it by chance.

> 11. *Whether she didn't bring death among the sheep through sorcery,*
> Says, and asks who told that to the magistrate, she was not guilty.

Both the aforesaid *instrumenta* were tightened a bit on both shins and loosened again. After that *Inquisitin* confessed that a planet reader[4] was there in Harxbüttel, who by her own assertion had had a miscarriage and could only

---

1 A *Mühlenpfal* is an oak pole in the mill stream, used to measure water levels. Presumably he fell into the mill stream or was injured by the pole.

2 "As her own words said"

3 "Kleppersack" was a common local name for the Devil.

4 A fortune-teller.

get away from Harxbüttel for the first time on the 8th day after this past Whitsuntide. More than a year ago she had burned chervil roots, and sprinkled the same burnt roots in the morning in the field in front of *Inquisitin's* son's door and also in the pasture, so that the sheep should die from that, because the *Schafmeisterse* hadn't wanted to give the planet woman any sheep's milk.[1] But *Inquisitin* hadn't taken part in that, other than that she had brought the wood and lit the fire.

1 2. *Whether she didn't learn from the Evil Enemy that one is supposed to burn sheep to powder and to give that to the sheep to prevent them from dying,*
Says, yes, that happened a year ago in Harxbüttel on her son's farm, in the sheep stable, towards evening around St. Martin's day,[2] with the planet woman present.

13. *Whether she didn't conjure something into the left leg of Hennig Roleffes of Wenden,*
Says, there was a cavalryman from Lückstedt in Harxbüttel, who had /: *respectfully reported* :/ a disease around his buttocks, and the publican[3] also contracted it, and it wasn't sorcery.

14. *Whether she didn't say to the wife of Hans Vette, at the wedding of the sheep master, that she could lock and unlock and whether that doesn't happen through sorcery,*
Says, she said "raise,"[4] because if one doesn't raise animals, where would they come from.

15. *Whether she didn't conjure the evil things into Jürgen Roleffes's head, that he turned totally dense from that,*
Says, yes, she did that eight years ago.

16. *How did she do that, and from where did she get the evil things,*

---

1 The sheep master and his wife lived on Tempel Anneke's son's farm.
2 November 11.
3 The publican is Hans Harves, not Hennig Roleffes, so there is some confusion in this question and answer.
4 Tempel Anneke's original words here are "*auf und zu ziehen.*" The question asked whether she said "*auf- und zuschliessen.*" She is using the similarity in the sounds of the words to claim that she was misquoted.

Says, at that time she had two live salamanders or toads, which were brought to her by the black man, and which she kept in her room in a *Stupen* pot[1] *from which the legs were broken*, and she buried them under the door post under the sill of Roleffes's house, and said, when Jürgen Roleffes walks over that, the Devil will fly into his head.

17. *Whether six years ago she didn't let Autor Bahrnesdorff know where his lost horses and foals were,*
Says, she said /: *salva venia added* :/ he should take himself to the front of the wood, they are walking there, because Kleppersack told her that.

18. *How did she know that,*
Says, as *ad proxe praecedentem Artm.*

19. *Whether she didn't make a pact with the Evil Enemy, and accomplish the aforesaid deeds through his help,*
Says, yes, that is so, and she did that.

20. *How and in what form did the same come to her,*
Says, he came as a middle-sized man, that is, an average man, who had black hair and wore a black coat.

21. *Whether she didn't do damage to people and animals, or else fruits of the field,*
Says, people, cattle and sheep, but not fruits of the field, one shouldn't do that.

22. *How did she accomplish it every time, and whether the Evil Spirit directed her and taught her,*
Says, yes.

23. *Whether she fornicated with the same in unnatural ways, how often, and in which place,*
Says, when he came the first time to her in the cow stable, she was supposed to lie with him, only she said, beforehand she must know more about it. A year later he came back to her again, and pursued her, he

---

1 A *Stupen* pot is one in which powder, and specifically medical or magical powder, is ground. See, for example, *Stuppe* in Lexer (1888/1995).

came to her more often, and had intercourse with her on her bed, and what came from him was cold, and the act, *congressus*,[1] didn't last very long.

24. *Whether she accomplished the evil things through these means,*
Says, those were the salamanders, she carried them[2] for nine days, then they came out, one at a time, she must have got them from Satan, as she had testified earlier, that she got the two salamanders or toads from Satan, that is to say, that he brought them.

25. *Whether she didn't bewitch the animals of Hans Wolter, the current swineherd in Bechtsbüttel, while the same still stayed in Harxbüttel, so that they died,*
Says, no, she didn't bewitch the animals, but she found a pot in the heather near the red *Rihe*,[3] which she wanted to throw into the water. Only her Kleppersack came, and he didn't want that, but said, the son of the swineherd had called her an old whore, so she should carry the pot to him, which she had then done. But she didn't carry this same pot to the front of the door but to a ditch, where there was nice grass, where the swineherd's cows were grazing, and one after the other died away. If the pot, in which there were five salamanders, had stayed there in the heather, all the animals would have died.[4] *Inquisitin* had found this pot by chance, and it was put there by somebody else.

26. *Whether she didn't bewitch the left leg of the son of the same swineherd,*
Says, yes, she sent two things into him by saying, "Fly in there." Because the boy had called her a whore.

27. *Whether she didn't give a pear, prepared through witchcraft, to the swineherd's son, and to what end did she do this,*
Says, she pulled out the stem, and blew into it three times, then the pear turned black inside, and she said therewith, "When you eat this, /: *God be with us* :/ the Devil shall fly into your body," but the boy didn't eat the pear.

---

1 "Coming together," sexual intercourse.
2 This implies that she was pregnant with them. See Folio 29, answers 15 and 16, pp. 108-09.
3 We could not find a translation for this word.
4 Since there was common grazing on the heather, this implies that everyone's cattle would have died.

28. *Whether she didn't bewitch Heinrich Cordes's child,*
    Says, no. Because the child had worms and a thick stomach.

But when she was talked to seriously she confessed that the *Martensche* of Wenden had bewitched the child, and she, *Inquisitin*, took it away from the child again, and three things came from the child, which she, *Inquisitin*, kept for three days under a bush, then she sent the same into a one-year-old calf belonging to a man called Engelke Poppe of Wenden, because the things wanted to eat.

29. *Whether she didn't bring it about through witches's arts that a black thing appeared to the child which wanted to get the child,*
    Says, when the things pinched the child in that way, it seemed to the same to be a black man.

Asked, *to whom had she taught sorcery?*
Says, first she taught it to a woman, Marie Eggeling of Ribbesbüttel, then a woman from Ohnhorst, the *Balmännsche*, also the *Gliemannsche* of Warmbüttel, and Hennig Meyer of Calberlah.

Asked, *was she still bound to Satan?*
Says, yes, she promised herself to the same for 12 years, one is still missing, she to still wanted to stand by him for that time, after that she wanted to return to the dear God.

Folio 29

[According to the Carolina, confessions obtained under torture can be used as the basis of a judgment in criminal law only if they are repeated "voluntarily," that is, without torture. Thus the questions in Folio 27 are presented to Tempel Anneke once again but without the presence of the executioner.]

The repeated confession without torture of *Inquisitin*, Anna Roleffes, otherwise called Tempel Anneke—in the presence of the court without the inclusion or introduction of the executioner, or the instruments belonging to torture—and what she added in her answer to one or the other *Articul*.

The 26th of October *Anno* 1663

Actum in the municipal jail of Hagen the 26th of October 1663.

By the honourable Gabriel Oeding, officer of the court, also Johann Velhagen and Otto Theune, both magistrates of the court, and Johann Pilgram, the court scribe.

The *Inquisitin* was confronted again today with her confession, given after the recent torture on October the 22nd regarding the *Inquisitionales* composed in *Act. Num.* 27—without the presence of the executioner—and the same also now confesses voluntarily as follows:

Ad.

1. *Where did she learn, that she could see from the sparks of fire a man's poverty, and the number of his children,*
   Says, as before, and after she is shown her previous testimony again *ad hunc Artm*[1] she stayed consistently with it, and added this to it, that the fifth spark, the black one /: *God be with us* :/ was the Devil, and from this same she was able to notice that the thief had to be a poor man.

She does not deny the further question asked at that time,[2] now as before.

---

1   "With respect to this article."
2   See Folio 28, following Question 1.

She wailed and cried, saying that she is sorry with all her heart about her sin, wanted heartily to repent, cried that what she did was only monkey business or monkey games.

2. *Whether she didn't conjure an injury into the thigh of Hans Harves of Harxbüttel, because one day he didn't want to have beer sent to her,*
Says consistently, she is not guilty of it, and repeats her recent testimony of the 22nd of October *Ad 10. Artm.*

3. *How she brought this about,*
Cessat.

4. *Whether Hennig Vaddrian, of Knochenhauer Street in Hagen, once came to her because of such an injury,*
Says as before *ad hunc Artm.*, she didn't hear that he said anything to her.

5. *Whether Harves didn't let her be told through the same that he had his injury from nobody but her,*
Says as before, she didn't hear that, otherwise she would have wanted to answer the charge.

6. *Whether Harves didn't threaten her, that if she would not take his injury away, he wanted to look elsewhere,*
Repeats her previous answer.

7. *Whether he didn't add, that if she were innocent, she should come and answer the charge,*
Repeats her previous answer *ad hunc Artm.*

8. *From whom had she learned her arts and especially the sorcery,*
Repeats, her recent testimony *ad hunc Artm.* contained in *Actus Num 28*, and adds, how she accepted the herbs from the man in the belief that he had more of this, and wanted to give her the same, because he said, "Look there." But he grabbed with his cold hand, and put the same in her hand, which terrified her so much that she took ill, and she had a sensation as if she were cold, because of that she lay on the bed. When then the man returned on the third day after, specifically in the night, he fell onto her body with the same hands, and didn't say anything, and

took her by the throat—after she had awoken from his arrival—as if he wanted to wring her neck, because of that she wanted to scream, but she couldn't because of her great fear. This way she first noticed that it wasn't right, and because of that the following morning she told her brother Hennig, since deceased, in what fear she had been through the night, only the brother didn't respond. And that time the man slipped away from her in silence, also that in her fear she didn't feel what else he had done with her.

9. *Whether she didn't conjure something into the left arm of Hans Harves's wife,*
Says, no, that was a temporary paralysis.

10. *Whether she didn't throw the head of a dead cow in the water near Harxbüttel to the end that when Hans Harves rowed across it his leg would be damaged,*
Repeats her earlier testimony.

11. *Whether she didn't bring death among the sheep through sorcery,*
Repeats her confession that she fetched wood and lit a fire, otherwise she didn't add anything to the affair.

12. *Whether she didn't learn from the Evil Enemy that one is supposed to burn sheep to powder and to give that to the sheep to prevent them from dying,*
Repeats her previous testimony, in *Art. Num. 28. Ad hunc Artm.*

13. *Whether she didn't conjure something into the left leg of Hennig Roleffes of Wenden,*
Repeats again her previous testimony.

14. *Whether she didn't say to the wife of Hans Vette, at the wedding of the sheep master, that she could lock and unlock, and whether that doesn't happen through sorcery,*
Says, the talk was about calves, that is why she said "raise."

15. *Whether she didn't conjure the evil things into Jürgen Roleffes's head, that he turned totally stupid from that,*
Says, she didn't bewitch him, Roleffes, otherwise she would have had to send the things into his head. Instead she put the things—there were

two things, and they had come from her through fornication with the Devil—in a small pot in the name of the Devil under the hollow front door sill, under which some earth had fallen away, so that aforesaid Roleffes should walk over them and become lame, through which he also got it in the head, although he improved to the extent that he was able to herd calves and oxen.

16. *How did she do that, and from where did she get the evil things,*
Repeats her current testimony *ad proxe praecedentem Artm.* as before, and corrects her given confession from before *ad hunc Artm.*, in that the things had come from her and had not been brought to her in the beginning by the black man.

17. *Whether six years ago she didn't let Autor Bahrensdorff know where his lost horses and foals were,*
Repeats her previous testimony, and adds, if the foals had not been with the horses the thief would probably have wanted to send the horses on, that is, to have brought them to a different place.

18. *How did she know that,*
Says, the Evil Enemy told her, that he had always been after her, and incited her,[1] even though she didn't always see his shape.

19. *Whether she didn't make a pact with the Evil Enemy, and accomplish the afore-said deeds through his help,*
Says, yes, she did that, and what happened, happened with his help.

20. *How and in what form did the same come to her,*
Repeats her previous testimony, and he was as cold as ice, so that she was terrified when he wanted to come to her. With this *Inquisitin* started to cry bitterly, saying, "Dear God, dear God, what have I done."

21. *Whether she didn't do damage to people and animals, or else fruits of the field,*
Says, she did damage to people, cattle and sheep, as confessed *ad hunc Artm.*, only she killed neither people nor animals.

---

1   The German, *"und ihr zugeblasen,"* means literally, "and blew to her."

22. *How did she accomplish it every time, and whether the Evil Spirit directed her and taught her,*
    Says, the Evil Spirit told her that she must do it.

23. *Whether she fornicated with the same in unnatural ways, how often, and in which place,*
    Repeats her previous testimony *ad hunc Artm.* That each time it happened on her bed. Even though she wanted to have a maid with her, nobody wanted to sleep with her, and not every time did something follow afterward, when she had intercourse with him.

24. *Whether she accomplished the evil things through these means,*
    Says as before, as happened *ad hunc Artum.* in *Act. Num 28.*

25. *Whether she didn't bewitch the cattle of Hans Wolter, the current swineherd in Bechtsbüttel, while the same still stayed in Harxbüttel, so that they died,*
    Repeats her most recent testimony *ad hunc Artm.*

26. *Whether she didn't bewitch the left leg of the son of the same swineherd,*
    Says, yes, she sent two things into his leg as told earlier.

27. *Whether she didn't give a pear, prepared through witchcraft, to the swineherd's son, and to what end did she do this,*
    Repeats her previous testimony *ad hunc Artm.*

Inquisitin behaves wretchedly and cries that God wanted to forgive her the sin, she would gladly mend her ways. Also, she didn't want to let herself be deceived again, in all her living days, as alas had happened, by the *Martensche*, the evil woman.

28. *Whether she didn't bewitch Heinrich Cordes's child,*
    Says, no, and repeats what she had previously testified to that.

29. *Whether she didn't bring it about through witches's arts that a black thing appeared to the child which wanted to get the child,*
    Says, yes, the child had two bad things, *Satanas* brought them through *Inquisitin*, so that if the child had died from that / : *since Satanas had done*

it :/ she would not have to take the child's sin upon herself. But she sent the things away from the child again and into a calf, as she had previously testified *ad* 28 *Artm*. But the child and its parents perished during the last plague in Rühme.[1]

Folio 30

[In this document the court formulates a set of questions concerning the details of Tempel Anneke's alleged relations with the Devil.]

Further *Articuli Inquisitionales*, about which *Inquisitin* is to be questioned without torture

1. Where, in what place, and in which way did she form a pact with the Devil,

2. What people, with the same powers as she, together with her, used sorcery, and what are the names of the same,

3. To whom did she teach witchcraft or sorcery here in town, or also out of town, in other places,

4. How and in which way did she accomplish that,

5. Whether, on her order, the same also did damage to people and animals,

6. Whether Satan didn't give her a mark, when she formed a pact with the same, and in what way did he give it to her,

7. In which place on her body can this sign be found, she should show that,

8. Whether she handled the Holy Communion and the Host indecently, what did she use them for, and on whose orders did she do that,

9. Whether she was also attacked by the Devil during the time she was here in prison,

10. How often was she on the Brocken,[1] after she formed a pact with the Evil Enemy, how did she get there, and what were her deeds there.

---

1 Brocken is a mountain in the Harz region near Brunswick where witches were believed to gather for the sabbath.

Folio 31

[Here Tempel Anneke answers the questions formulated in Folio 30.]

The answers given without torture by *Inquisitin* Anna Roleffes, otherwise called Tempel Anneke, to the further questions formulated in *Actis* 30.

The 27th of October *Anno* 1663

Actum in the municipal jail of Hagen

The 27th of October *Anno* 1663

By all of the persons of the court of the municipality of Hagen.

Inquisitin was interrogated without torture about the further questions formulated in *Actis. Num.* 30, and gave her answers to each, as follows:

Ad.

1. *Where, in what place, and in which way did she form a pact with the Devil,*
   Says, in Harxbüttel, on her son's farm in the granary, because the Evil Enemy, whom she came to know when she accepted the herbs from him, came to her the previous evening in her room in front of her bed, and ordered her to the granary. When she came to him at the particular time, indeed at night by the light of the moon, she had to step into a circle on the ground which was black, and on his urging, she let three small drops of blood into a small piece of linen, from her smallest finger on her right hand, which she had pricked with a needle, and she had to give it to him. Thereupon he had started and said, "I now have your blood, now you are mine, with body and blood, now you shall do what I want from you." As she now answered, "Nevertheless, God sees more, or has more worth or more power," he had countered and said, "You are mine, and shall do what I want, you shall not again swallow what the pastor gives /: *while administering the sacrament* :/ neither the wine." Instead she should do with it what he told her to, therefore she then agreed to that, and she had to swear by holding her fingers upright and saying, "I forswear sun, moon and stars, and I will do everything."

With the further command that if someone were to appear at her place wanting something from her for a game of dice or cards, she should give him that which she kept in the small cloth.[1] And whereupon he would come, and he would want to hear about it from such a person himself. So it then happened, that several years ago, in Gardelegen she was at the table of the Lord, where she let the Host together with the received wine slip from her mouth into a small piece of cloth, and saved the same, and when she returned again from there to this region here, she sold it to Joseph Balmann, a tailor, who was born in Bechtsbüttel, and is now deceased, so that he could shoot reliably. She directed the said Balmann to go under the roof in front of the Wenden mill,[2] because the same came here to stay in Brunswick in N. Kohröwer's house *Am Graben*.[3] There the same Evil Enemy came, and made him pledge an oath with a handshake, because those who accept and use those Hosts must likewise belong to the Evil Enemy.

Then, seven years ago in Ahnbüttel, she had, as far as she remembers, let the Host and the received wine slip into a small piece of cloth when she stepped back from the altar and went back. Cordt Hesel of Hillerse, since deceased, got those from her for 12*g.*, so that he should be lucky in card games. This Hesel had to come to a bake house,[4] where *Inquisitin* directed him to go, where he had to pledge an oath to the Evil Spirit.

Third, several years ago, when the previous pastor was still at Wenden, at Communion, she had let the received Host and the wine slip from her mouth into a small piece of cloth. These Frantz N. had received from her for 9*g.*—and a rabbit, which he had promised to bring to her—so that he could shoot reliably. This one *Inquisitin* had directed to the thick bush in front of the Wenden Bridge, then the Evil One came and made him pledge himself to him.

For the fourth, four years ago, here in Brunswick in the St. Martini church, she had been to confession with the young priest, because at that time she was always with the old *Christsche* at the Altstadt Market. As she came the following day with others to the altar, and received the

---

1 The Host (see below on this page.).
2 The Wenden Mill was a water mill at the Wenden Gate. (See D on Map 2, p. xxi)
3 Wendengraben, street number 30 on the city plan, near the Wenden Gate.
4 This was a house to which people brought their bread to be baked.

Host as well as the wine, she had let both slip into a small piece of linen cloth, and she so kept it, until later on she came upon Hans Bündtge, the marksman. She sold it to the same for an Ortstaler so that when he shot he could hit the target reliably. Inquisitin had directed this Bündtge to go under the wooden arch in front of the Altstadt beer cellar. There the Evil One also came to that place, and made him pledge himself to him. She hadn't misused the Lord's Supper more than that, because in twelve years she hadn't been more often than that to the table of the Lord, also she taught no one else.

2. *What people, with the same powers as she, together with her, used sorcery, and what are the names of the same,*
Says, she didn't know of anyone else. Except in Vordorf there was one, called the *Epgerse*, who is still alive, and she was the master of *Inquisitin*, that is, had more knowledge than *Inquisitin*.

3. *To whom did she teach sorcery here in town, or also out of town, in other places,*
Says, here in the city she didn't know of anyone, also she didn't teach anyone, but outside she had given instruction on how they should help sick animals and people with cooked herbs, in Ribbesbüttel Marie Eggeling, then of Abbesbüttel N.N. a farmer whose wife had a mark on her cheek, and Hans Ulenhaut of Wasbüttel, as also Margarethe Schwartz of Warmbüttel, then Margarethe Holland of Gifhorn, but no others. But on how she stood with the Evil Enemy, and what she did in his name, she didn't teach anyone else. Why would she come to accuse people, of whom she had no proof.

4. *How and in which way did she accomplish that,*
Cessat.

5. *Whether, on her order, the same didn't also do damage to people and cattle,*
Cessat.

6. *Whether Satan didn't give her a mark, when she formed a pact with the same, and in what way did he give it to her,*
Says, yes, because as she came to the granary, as reported above, he wanted to give her a sign under her face, only she didn't want to have that. Because of that he grabbed her by the left knee, and put a sign onto

her, she didn't know with what, in which something like a small coral could be seen.

Thereupon she showed the exposed knee in which on the outside, right above the kneecap, a small scar was visible, as if pushed into it with a finger. But when such a scar was actually looked at by the executioner /: *who did not touch her anywhere else, neither did he do anything else, except that he looked at this sign, and was supposed to give his opinion :/*, it was found that it was a considerable scar, as big as one could push in with a finger, but there was no mark like a coral to be seen in the same. So the executioner could give no other *Indicium*,[1] except that it looked like a wound or smallpox scar, which had mostly grown over again.

7. *In which place on her body, can this sign be found, she should show that,*
   Says, as in the previous *Articul*, that the scar on the left knee was the sign.

8. *Whether she handled the Holy Communion and the Host indecently, what did she use them for, and on whose orders did she do that,*
   Says, as above *ad Artm* paragraph 2 *circa mediam*.[2]

9. *Whether she was also attacked by the Devil during the time she was here in prison,*
   Says, no, no.

10. *How often was she on the Brocken, after she formed a pact with the Evil Enemy, how did she get there, and what were her deeds there,*
    Says, after she made a pact with the Evil One, she went yearly to Walpurgis Night[3] on a male goat, which Tilke[4] brought, and travelled there with the same. There she held a light in her hand, like three others who were not the oldest, the others however danced. After that they received *Ordinant* /: *the words used by Inquisitin* :/ what they were supposed to do, namely if someone came, and wanted help from them, they should kill everything, especially people and animals, which she for her part had not done.

---

1   "Indication."
2   "Near the middle." See the second paragraph of her answer to Question 1, p. 114.
3   Walpurgis Night is the eve of May 1, when witches were believed to gather on the Brocken.
3   Til Kleppersack, i.e., the Devil.

Folio 32

[This folio contains a further set of questions, focusing more closely on the pact with the Devil.]

Further *Articuli* about which Anna Roleffes, otherwise called Tempel Anneke, is to be interrogated without torture, yet seriously;

---

1. Whether she didn't offer up to Satan the Costly Sacrifice[1] of our Lord and Saviour, Jesus Christ, the Holy Trinity, the Holy Sacrament of Baptism, and the entire Christian teachings: and swear to be his own, and had to pledge herself with an oath,

2. In which place, and at what time, during the day or night did this take place,

3. With which formal acts and words did she really do this,

4. Whether she spoke them from herself or did the Devil prompt her and she repeated after him one word after the other, or in some other way repeated, and pledged herself,

5. Whether she didn't have to pledge herself to Satan, with body as well as soul, and completely surrender herself through a sworn oath,

6. Whether she caught her blood in a small cloth, and gave it as a pledge to her lover, called Kleppersack,

7. Whether she didn't bind herself further with Satan, and in which form,

8. Whether, and in what manner,—when she didn't carry out the order he gave to her, which she received yearly at the witches's dance and had to pledge herself to the heresy—Satan treated her badly, beat her and tortured her until she herself, or through others like her, had to perpetrate it,

---

1   I.e, the Crucifixion

9. Whether she didn't have to swear every year, specifically during the witches's dance, with an oath to commit herself to carry out Satan's order,

10. What the oath sounds like verbatim, and in which form did she each year consistently swear,

11. Whether she didn't also know Hans Hoyer from Sickte, cowherd there and in Wenden, and his wife Anne Holsten from Gardelegen,

12. Through what did she make their aquaintance, and how long did they cultivate it together,

13. Whether they didn't commit sorcery, and did harm to people and animals in the fields and pastures,

14. How long, and in which places, and on whose initiative and orders did they commit these things against animals and people,

15. Who had taught this to whom, and in what place.

Folio 33

[There are two parts to the proceedings recorded here. First, Tempel Anneke answers the questions formulated in Folio 32. After the interrogation, the court searches for the witch's mark, which Tempel Anneke confessed to having received from the Devil in Folio 31.]

Voluntary confession of *Inquisitin* regarding the further *Articulos* contained in *Actis Num.* 32., including further exploration of the witch's mark of *Inquisitin*, and the report of the barber concerning this.

The 4th of November *Anno* 1663

Actum in the municipal jail of Hagen

The 4th of November *Anno* 1663

By the appointed persons of the court of the municipality Hagen.

Inquisitin is interrogated without torture about the further *Articulos* formulated in *Actis Num.* 32., and gave as her answer voluntarily on each one *formalibus verbis*, as follows:

Ad.

1. *Whether she didn't offer up to Satan the Costly Sacrifice of our Lord and Saviour, Jesus Christ, the Holy Trinity, the Holy Sacrament of Baptism, and the entire Christian teachings: and swear to be his own, and had to pledge herself with an oath,*

   Says purely, yes, to all and each of the *commata*[1] of this *Articul* and the content expressed in them. She behaved wretchedly, saying, there would be mercy with God and the authorities, they would be able to be merciful to her.

2. *In which place, and at what time, during the day or night did this take place,*

   Says, she barely knows anymore. But when she was reminded without

---

1   Points.

torture, she said in the granary, in the evening, when it began to get dark, after the sun went to rest.

3. *With which formal acts and words did she really do this,*
Says, she said she would be his /: Satan's :/.

Acts miserably with crying and hand wringing, reporting that the pastors had consoled her well the previous day, and he /: Satan :/ did not come to her, was not allowed to be with her.

4. *Whether she spoke them from herself or did the Devil prompt her: and she repeated after him one word after the other, or in some other way repeated, and pledged herself,*
Says, she had to repeat after Satan, that she would be his, because he had prompted her, "You shall renounce sun, moon, and stars, and you will be my own being," with that she had sworn.
Inquisitin wails and shouts "Oh, oh, oh, oh, what did I do, that I have allowed myself to be led astray by Satan in this way, oh, oh, oh."

5. *Whether she didn't have to pledge herself to Satan, with body as well as soul, and completely surrender herself through a sworn oath,*
Says purely, yes. But started to moan, saying with God there is mercy, he would not leave her with Satan, "Oh, oh, oh, I will not despair."

6. *Whether she caught her blood in a small cloth, and gave it as a pledge to her lover, called Kleppersack,*
Says, yes, yes. Because he had wanted a sign from her, so she gave him the small drops of blood.

7. *Whether she didn't bind herself further with Satan, and in which form,*
Says, no, never and nowhere else but in the granary.

8. *Whether, and in what manner—when she didn't carry out the order he gave to her, which she received yearly at the witches's dance and had to pledge herself to the heresy—Satan treated her badly, beat her and tortured her until she herself, or through others like her, had to perpetrate it,*
Says, he had told each one separately what she was supposed to do, and

had they accomplished all of that, evil would have come out of it. Even though *Inquisitin* didn't hear what the other witches were ordered, nor did the other witches hear what *Inquisitin* was ordered, nonetheless she had not performed everything that she was ordered, for she had killed no people, because otherwise she would have committed even greater sin. And even though he treated her badly with pinching when she didn't want to perform everything, and specifically not doing damage to people, in spite of that he didn't beat her, and she had in no way instructed others like her do that or perform that.

God forgives murderers and manslaughterers their sins, he would forgive *Inquisitin* her sin as well.

9. *Whether she didn't have to swear every year, specifically during the witches's dance, with an oath to commit herself to carry out Satan's order,*

Says, yes, she did swear that, but hadn't done it, that is to say, not everything, because she was supposed to kill all the time, that is, constantly, but she had not done that. What she did, she had already confessed.

10. *What the oath sounds like verbatim, and in which form did she each year consistently swear,*

Says, he had prompted: "Forswear body and soul, that you will do what I tell you." Thereupon she had lifted two fingers of her right hand, and said: "Now I will be yours with body and soul, and will do what you tell me." And it happened every year that way, and he didn't do anything new, that is, as she explained it, he had or used no other kind of words. She, however, wasn't obedient to him, in that she killed no people, but only committed that which she has already confessed.

She thanked the dear God, that she has escaped him. The dear God will be merciful to her, that will be with her in life or in death. She thanks God that it came to this, and that she was brought to her repentance.

Ad.

11. *Whether she didn't also know Hans Hoyer from Sickte, cowherd there and in Wenden, and his wife Anne Holsten from Gardelegen,*

Says, she does not know these two people. Why should she conceal that or hide that. Says consistently, no.

1 2. *Through what did she make their acquaintance, and how long did they cultivate it together,*
Cessat.

1 3. *Whether they didn't commit sorcery, and did it to people and cattle in the fields and pastures,*
Cessat.

1 4. *How long, and in which places, and on whose initiative and orders did they commit these things against cattle and people,*
Cessat.

1 5. *Who had taught this to whom, and in what place,*
Cessat.

Even though at *finito Examine*[1] it was put to *Inquisitin* that she had reported her mark and that there was a coral to be found in it. While she had a scar on her left knee, the coral was not to be found there. And she should be aware of this, and if she had another mark on her body or in her clothes, she should voluntarily indicate this and confess to it. Yet she stood consistently by the assertion, that the scar on the knee of her left leg shown earlier was her mark, because he had given it to her when she had to swear. The coral was grown into it; in the beginning, when it was pinched, what was in it was nothing other than a coral.

Hereupon[2] the barber Master Johann Sellenstedt was called for, who then—by the power of the instructions given into his hand—not only looked upon the frequently mentioned mark but also /: *after he had seen or felt nothing like a coral or what could be comparable to the same, and after which her eyes were bound with a handkerchief by the bailiff* :/ he examined and felt the scar as the indicated mark on the knee with a fine iron *Instrumentum*, and he inserted the iron several times forcefully. But because of the hard skin with which this mark was covered and hardened it did not penetrate nor did it cause *Inquisitin* pain, so that she didn't say anything or complain about severe pain. He also poked about a hand's width around the mark with the previous *Instrumento*,

---

1   "End of the examination."

2   The scribe, Johann Pilgram, appears to have considerable difficulty with this section, since there are numerous corrections, inserts, and marginal additions, which are unusual for him.

and asked her if she felt this. And as she said, yes, that hurts me everywhere where you pricked now, thereupon the barber held the *Instrumentum* again fairly hard onto the mark, so that, according to his report, the previously mentioned thick skin, in the place where he inserted the *Instrumentum*, as it were, went into the flesh under the thick skin with the *Instrumento* ....[1] Only *Inquisitin* felt no pain, and didn't complain about that, that she felt pain, as she had done before when her flesh around the scar was examined, at that time she quickly started to say that it hurt her.

Herewith *Inquisitin* was discharged from the interrogation room, and is brought back again to the jail cell, well secured and locked.[2]

---

1   This sentence was left unfinished.
2   This means that the leg irons were fastened again to her legs.

Folio 34

[This document contains copies of letters sent to Gifhorn, and to Thune in the district of Neubrück, in which the court seeks confirmation of aspects of Tempel Anneke's confessions in Folio 28.]

Requisitoriales in Subsid.

To the regional civil administrator and civil officer of Gifhorn
and the civil officer of Neubrück
together with included *Interrogatorii*
sent on the 5th and 6th of 9bris

To the civil officer and bailiff of Gifhorn

Most nobly born, powerful, strong also knightly, much respected and well-learned, especially most honoured gentlemen and friends.

First our willing offer of service, it cannot be withheld from the same, in which manner, Anna Roleffes, otherwise called Tempel Anneke—who came under suspicion because of her sorcery, and because of that has been held captive until now—confessed and testified amongst other things during the previous *inquisition*, how she accomplished her witches's work on the persons specified below and sometimes their animals. However, since we require the true information about that, so herewith the most honourable, powerful gentlemen, also much respected officers are respectfully requested, once more to assist us *in subsidium Juris*, and to interrogate each person specified below:

1. Whether, 5 or 6 years ago now, the left leg of Hans Köhler of Vollbüttel went away, that is, disappeared, even though it did not cause him any pain,

2. Whether approximately ten years ago, the brown horse of Til Schwartz from Leiferde in Papenteich—with which at that time he had run over Anna Roleffes otherwise called Tempel Anneke—fell over and died,

Item, whether the same fell into a mill pole two years ago?

3. Whether the animals of Hans Wolter, the current swineherd in Bechtsbüttel, when he still lived in Harxbüttel about 5 years ago, were bewitched so that one after the other died away,

4. Whether the left leg of the same swineherd's son wasn't bewitched, and what it felt like,

5. Whether Anna Roleffes, otherwise called Tempel Anneke, gave a pear to the same swineherd's son at that time, what was it like on the outside and inside,

Item, what did he do with it, and what happened to him and befell him afterwards?

Now what each specified person will say, regarding that which concerns them, their precise answer, or other news. Unless, due to other obligations, the officers don't have time to find out the truth, we expect them to kindly refer the same to us. We look forward with anticipation to hearing, and we are willing and offering to repay in kind in the same or other circumstances. We, on both sides, recommend ourselves to the powerful protection of God.

Done thus, in Brunswick, the 5th of November *Anno* 1663

To the most noble, powerful, also knightly, most respected gentlemen.

The willing court officers and magistrates of the municipality of Hagen in that very place.

To Joh. Gürn, civil officer of Thune

Knightly, much respected and well-learned, especially good friend.

After offering our greetings and friendly wishes, it cannot be withheld from the same, in which manner, Tempel Anneke, notorious through her magical works, in her confession amongst other things also confessed and made this known, that Engelke Poppe in Wenden had a calf 6 years ago to which she sent the evil things, and in effect bewitched it. As we would like to have definite information about that and desire to know the truth, our further request for assistance again reaches the bailiff, so that he may again call Engelke Poppe to appear before him, and interrogate the same *gravia admonitione de veritate dicenda*.

Whether a calf of Engelke Poppe in Wenden wasn't bewitched, and when did this happen,

Item, whether the calf died through magical works, and in which way and manner did the dying occur? What the answer to this will be we will hopefully soon learn. We are offering the civil officer for this instance to willingly repay with the same or other desired services. Given in Brunswick the 6th of November *Anno* 1663. {...}[1]

---

1   The signature following has been cut off.

Folio 35

[This is a reply received from Gifhorn to the letter contained in Folio 34.]

Principality of Lüneburg, Gifhorn office
sent the 7th 9bris 1663

The letter received here from the court officials of Hagen of the city of Brunswick, by which it is asked {...}, the people recently summoned shall be interrogated in the desired way, and their testimony will be forwarded {...} insofar as this sheds light.

Gifhorn the 7th 9bris 1663

Folio 36

[This folio contains the testimony of Ernst Poppe in reply to the questions formulated in Folio 34.]

To be officially submitted to the appointed court officers and magistrates of the municipality of Hagen

---

The given testimony of Ernst Poppe
District office of Neubrück
The 9th 9bris 1663
Received the 14th 9bris 1663

Actum in the district office of Neubrück
The 9th 9bris 1663

According to the appointed court officers and magistrates of the municipality of Hagen, in Brunswick, it was reported here on the 6th of this month, in what manner Tempel Anneke, notorious for her magical works, in her confession among other things also said this and that, that Ernst Poppe of Wenden had a calf six years ago, into which she sent the evil things, and in effect bewitched it. Since the gentlemen indicated now very much want certainty, the same wish to request *subsidiaris* the currently appointed civil officer to interrogate the aforementioned Poppe, and specifically *gravia admonitione*,

1. *Whether years ago a calf of Ernst Poppe of Wenden was bewitched, and when did this happen,*

   Item whether the calf died of magical works, and in which way did the dying occur?

In the pursuance of this, Ernst Poppe was summoned early in the morning, and after previous severe interrogation the same testified that (1) he recalled in what manner a calf fell in 1657 at his farm in Wenden, which over several weeks was fed in the best possible way in order to raise it; how this didn't help the same, but rather it went mad and thus because of its death did not fatten, and they sold it for 12mrg. But whether (2) it was bewitched he could not really know, nor say, even though it was seen in that way, after Tempel Anneke was frequently in and out of his house. *Actum ut supra*.

Johann Gürn

Folio 37

[This folio contains the report from Gifhorn that was promised in Folio 35.]

All the most knightly, most respected and well learned officers of the court and magistrates of the court in the municipality of Hagen in the city of Brunswick, especially my much esteemed gentlemen and valued friends.

Received 18th 9bris 1663

Most knightly, most respected and well learned, especially very powerful gentlemen and valued friends, at whose request the wife of the swineherd of Bechtsbüttel appeared here, and was questioned about the forwarded points. What she testified to is apparent in the attachment.[1] She was encouraged to speak the truth in the report done for the gentlemen. The other two[2] were also summoned, but were not to be found either in Vollbüttel or in Leiferde. If the same are now present in other villages and {...}, they will also be summoned, questioned, and their testimony will be forwarded. {...}

To my very powerful gentlemen,

Martin Bregen
Gifhorn the 12th 9bris 1663

---

1   This testimony is filed as Folio 39.
2   Hans Köhler and Til Schwartz.

Folio 38

[This document is a draft copy of the first part of Folio 34. It appears without a cover, address, or date.]

Most nobly born, powerful and strong also knightly and well-learned, especially most honoured gentleman and neighbourly friend.

First our willing offer of service, it cannot be withheld from the same, in which manner, Anna Roleffes, otherwise called Tempel Anneke—who came under suspicion because of her sorcery, and because of that has been held captive until now—confessed and testified amongst other things during the previous inquisition, how she accomplished her witches's work on the persons specified below and sometimes their animals. However, since we require the true information about that, so herewith the most honourable, powerful gentlemen, also much respected officers are respectfully requested, once more to assist us *in subsidium Juris*, and to interrogate each person specified below:

1. Whether, 5 or 6 years ago now, the left leg of Hans Köhler of Vollbüttel went away, that is, disappeared, even though it did not cause him any pain?

2. Whether approximately ten years ago, the brown horse of Til Schwartz from Leiferde in Papenteich—with which at that time he had run over Anna Roleffes otherwise called Tempel Anneke—fell over and died, *Item*, whether the same fell into a mill pole two years ago,

3. Whether the animals of Hans Wolter, the current swineherd in Bechtsbüttel, when he still lived in Harxbüttel about 5 years ago, were bewitched so that one after the other died away,

4. Whether the left leg of the same swineherd's son wasn't bewitched, and what it felt like,

5. Whether Anna Roleffes, otherwise called Tempel Anneke, gave a pear to the same swineherd's son at that time, what was it like on the outside and inside,

Item, what did he do with it, and what happened to him and befell him afterwards?

Folio 39

[This is the testimony of Anna Timmerman, which was attached to the report from Gifhorn in Folio 37.]

Testimony of the swineherd woman of Bechtsbüttel

Testimony of the wife of Hans Wolter and of their son, residents of Bechtsbüttel

Received the 18th 9bris 1663

Actum in Gifhorn, the 11th of November *Anno* 1663

Hans Wolter, now of Bechtsbüttel, was requested here, because of the wishes of the officials of the court in Hagen in the city of Brunswick. As he could not appear due to age, his wife presented herself with her son, and was questioned about the points sent here and reports on them as follows.

Ad art.

3. *Whether the animals of Hans Wolter, the current swineherd in Bechtsbüttel, when he still lived in Harxbüttel about 5 years ago, were bewitched so that one after the other died away,*

Says that 8 years ago, when she was still in Harxbüttel, her son had played together with other children in the sand outside the village. Tempel Anneke came by and grabbed her son by the head and made him walk in a circle so that he fell to the ground. Whereupon the boy said, "You old whore, why don't you go to the Tempel[1] and let us children play." To which Tempel Anneke said, "You'll regret that." Soon after, three days later, first a cow suddenly died away on her. After half a fortnight, two more heads, after that a pig. When the animals were dead, her son became ill, he got it in the knee, for which she used many remedies but nothing wanted to help.

---

1   I.e., the Tempel pub.

Ad.

4. *Whether the left leg of the same swineherd's son wasn't bewitched, and what it felt like,*

Says, her son got the damage into the leg, was lying down for a long time, she used various remedies but it helped little. Tempel Anneke often came to the boy and visited in her absence, for what reasons she didn't know. One time her husband came in and found her in the house. He spoke to her, if she wanted to help his son or not, took up the battle axe and was willing to chop one of her arms off, but she ran away, and didn't comment. She left the village and stayed away for nine weeks. Also she had said several times that the boy will not die from the affliction,

Ad.

5. *Whether Anna Roleffes, otherwise called Tempel Anneke, gave a pear to the same swineherd's son at that time, what was it like on the outside and inside,*

Says, as did the boy, who was also present, when he had the damage in the leg for fourteen days Tempel Anneke came to him when he was alone in the house and offered him a pear, which he didn't want to accept from her, whereupon she put the same in a pot on the fireplace. Now when her daughter came from the garden and saw the pear, she said to the boy, "There is a pear lying here," took the same out and gave it to him, which he took. On the outside it was good to look at, but when he bit into it, and got some of it into his body, it was very bitter, also there were black marks visible in it, whereupon he immediately got great pains in his body, so that he could not rest anywhere. She fetched something from the apothecary and brewed it for him. Also consulted with the pastor in Garbsen about this, who also gave her something which she brewed for him, until finally the good God made it that the pain in the body stilled itself. After that the leg also came a bit more right again. But the knee cap was mostly eaten away by worms, so that five bones fell out off it. While she could not say that Tempel Anneke did that to him, the conjecture was great. She repeats her testimony previously given in Brunswick in front of the officials of the court. And she puts everything in the hands of God and the court.

The other two, Hans Köhler supposedly in Vollbüttel and Til Schwartz supposedly in Leiferde, while they had been summoned, in both villages nobody of such name was found. And because no one else knew anything specific to report about Tempel Anneke, except that she was thought to be suspicious, one had to leave it at that.

Actum ut supra.

Martin Bregen

Folio 40

[Here the mother and brother of Jürgen Roleffes are questioned concerning his alleged bewitching by Tempel Anneke, first mentioned in Folio 2. The late date of this document may be because the interrogation of Jürgen's mother, Magdalena Bösken, followed a decree by the cathedral chapter of St. Blasius. This decree may have been required because she lived within the legal jurisdiction of the church.]

The report given by Heinrich Roleffes's widow and her son Hennig Roleffes, concerning the bewitching of their son and brother respectively.

The 28th of November *Anno* 1663

Actum in the municipal jail of Hagen
the 28th of November *Anno* 1663

By the court officers and magistrates of the municipality of Hagen in Brunswick

Following the subsidiary decree of the canons of the chapter of St. Blasius[1] in Brunswick, Magdalena Bösken, the widow left behind by Heinrich Roleffes of Harxbüttel, is introduced, and after being carefully reminded to speak the truth, was questioned:

Whether Jürgen Roleffes was bewitched eight years ago so that he turned completely dense in the head?

To that she gave her reply with a sad heart and gestures, and said that Jürgen Roleffes was her bodily son, and was married about eight years ago now. And soon it appeared as if he had got the holy thing /: the Rose, St. Anthony's Fire[2] :/ in the head. Then sometimes it appeared to get better and sometimes worse, but later it got worse and worse and stayed like that, until he turned completely dense and got a lame hand. It was so bad with him, that he didn't know her, his own mother, and his own wife, because he often asked these two people where they were from. And all the time he was in such a

---

1 The cathedral church of St. Blasius.
2 Erysipelas. A bacterial infection of the skin causing redness and swelling.

bad way that it was pitiful, and she could not suppose otherwise than that it was sorcery. But who did it, God must know. Tempel Anneke, now sitting in captivity, asserted he was bewitched, and had wanted to help him, but pretended that it had been too long, and the time / : *to cure* : / was over. And when the oftmentioned Jürgen Roleffes, her son / : *salva venia* : / occasionally blew his nose, bones blew out of it.

Likewise Hennig Roleffes from Wenden, Jürgen Roleffes's bodily brother, is questioned about the *Interrogatorium* set out in the beginning *gravia admonitione de veritate dicenda*, and to that he answered, how eight years ago his brother, Jürgen Roleffes, was married on his farm in Harxbüttel, it had lasted about four weeks, then the misfortune began, that it so reigned or raged in his head that he could have no peace. He went far and wide because of that, but could get no advice without being told that it had been done to him in a bouquet or a little bunch of flowers when he smelled them. Because of that he, Jürgen Roleffes, and others were completely convinced that he was bewitched. And it got worse and worse with him after the bones fell out of his nose as reported before. He is still complaining all the time, and three years ago he became lame in his arm and leg as well. Also he was often heard to say that he could not lie down, but had to jump up, because it crunched so in his head as if something living were in it and ate. Whether *Inquisitin* Tempel Anneke had done it, he didn't know. But it is true that his brother Jürgen had seized Tempel Anneke's son's brother-in-law in the meadow, then 14 days later it had started to happen to him, as told before, so that he is now still dense, and a miserable human being, who is served nothing by his life.

Folio 41

[This document is the statement of the final confession to be obtained from Tempel Anneke. It is drafted by the *Syndicus*, Johann Baumgarten, and it is based on the decision received from the University of Jena contained in Folio 42.]

Decretum the 23rd 1obris 1663

The *Inquisitin* Anna Roleffes, otherwise called Tempel Anneke, is to be interrogated again without torture by the officers and magistrates of the court.

Whether she would consistently stand by it;

1. That she renounced the Costly Sacrifice of our Lord and Saviour Jesus Christ, the H.[1] Trinity, the H. Sacrament of Baptism, and the entire Christian doctrine, and swore to be Satan's own, and to submit to him,

2. That she received a mark from the same,

3. Learned sorcery,

4. Often abused the H. Host,

5. Visited the Devil's dances,

6. Fornicated unnaturally with the Evil Enemy,

7. Tortured the thief who stole from Tiehmann,

8. That the Evil Enemy went into Hans Köhler's leg according to her will, so that his leg wasted away,

9. That according to her direction one of Til Schwartz's horses died,

---

1   "Holy."

10. That she put the things in a small pot in the name of the Devil on Jürgen Roleffes's farm, so that the said Roleffes should walk over it and become lame, how then through that he also got it in the head,

11. That through the Evil Enemy whispering to her she gave news to Autor Bahrensdorff where his lost horses and foals were,

12. That on the bidding of her lover she carried a pot to a ditch where there was nice grass, where the cows of the current swineherd of Bechtsbüttel were grazing, from which one after the other died away,

13. That she sent two things into the leg of the son of the same swineherd,

14. That she removed the things from Heinrich Cordes's bewitched child and sent them into Engelke Poppe's calf.

Herewith the officers of the court and magistrates are ordered to write down carefully the repeated voluntary confession of the *Inquisitin*, and as soon as possible obtain it *ad Acta*.[1]

Decretum through the administration of justice of Jena, the 23rd of December *Anno* 1663

J.B. Baumgarten[2]

---

1   "For the legal record."

2   Johann Burchard Baumgarten, *Syndicus*.

Folio 42

[This is the second decision received from the legal faculty of the University of Jena. The faculty finds Tempel Anneke guilty of a set of specific accusations, on the basis of which the court in Brunswick formulates its final judgment.]

To the noble, honourable, highly- and well-learned, most and very wise mayors and officers of the city of Brunswick, our gracious gentlemen and friends.

Received from Jena 23rd 1obris *Anno* 1663

Offering our friendly services in advance, noble, honourable, highly- and well-learned, most and very wise, gracious gentlemen and friends.

Because earlier the same sent over to us the file of enquiry issued against Anna Roleffes, otherwise called Tempel Anneke, and requested our legal advice about it, we pronounce after careful reading and consideration of the law:

Said *Inquisitin* has admitted and confessed, that she renounced the Costly Sacrifice of our Lord and Saviour Jesus Christ, the H. Trinity, the H. Sacrament of Baptism, and the entire Christian doctrine, and swore to be Satan's own, and to submit to him, received a mark from the same, learned sorcery, often abused the Holy Host, visited the Devil's dances, fornicated unnaturally with the Evil Enemy, tortured the thief who stole from Tiehmann, and that the Evil Enemy went into Hans Köhler's leg according to her will, so that his leg wasted away, that in the same way according to her direction one of Til Schwartz's horses died. Further, that she put the things in a small pot in the name of the Devil on Jürgen Roleffes's farm, so that the said Roleffes should walk over it and become lame, how then through that he also got it in the head, also through the Evil Enemy whispering to her she gave news to Autor Bahrensdorff where his lost horses and foals were, on the bidding of her lover carried a pot to a ditch where there was nice grass, where the cows of the current swineherd of Bechtsbüttel were grazing, from which one after the other died away, and sent two things into the leg of the son of the same swineherd. How she removed the things from Heinrich Cordes's bewitched child and sent them into Engelke Poppe's calf.

If the same persists in her given confession before the supreme capital court, so because of the crimes committed and confessed to she will be condemned from life to death by fire.

Officially certified by law with our seal.
Ordinarius, Decanus, Senior and other *doctors* of the Faculty of Law at the University of Jena.

Folio 43

[This folio contains Tempel Anneke's final confession to the accusations formulated in Folio 41.]

The repeated confession of *Inquisitin* Anna Roleffes, otherwise called Tempel Anneke, without torture, to the contents of the questions contained in the *Decreto* in *Actis Num.* 41, whereby she intends to stand, also upon which she intends to live or die.

The 24th *Decembris Anno* 1663

Actum in the municipal jail of Hagen

The 24th *Decembris Anno* 1663

By the court officers and magistrates of the municipality of Hagen, here in Brunswick

Following the directions of the *Decreti* given on 23rd *hujus*[1] in *Actis Num.* 41, *Inquisitin* Anna Roleffes, otherwise called Tempel Anneke, was questioned again on this day without torture, whether she would stand consistently by that which is contained in the points mentioned below, and from first to last put before her clearly and distinctly, to which she answered *formalibus verbis* to each specifically as follows:

Ad.
   1. *That she renounced the Costly Sacrifice of our Lord and Saviour Jesus Christ, the H. Trinity, the H. Sacrament of Baptism, and the entire Christian doctrine, and swore to be Satan's own, and to submit to him,*
   Says, yes. But our Lord would forgive her her sin. She had /: until now :/ diligently prayed to him.

Ad.
   2. *That she received a mark from the same,*

---

1   Of this (month).

Says, yes, what she had said once she wanted to stand by consistently. And wished upon this, saying "Oh Lord Jesus Christ, stand by me and forgive all my sin."

Ad.

3. *Learned sorcery,*
   Says, yes.

Ad.

4. *Often abused the H. Host,*
   Says, yes. But she would /: *nevertheless* :/ still receive communion before she is to die. And would the court officers be compassionate with her the same as is our Father in Heaven.

Ad.

5. *Visited the Devil's dances,*
   Says, yes. What she had said she wanted to stand by consistently, to live and die by it, only now does she see what she has done, that she has committed great mortal sins.

Ad.

6. *Fornicated unnaturally with the Evil Enemy,*
   Says, yes. She did not want to turn her words around, but remain consistent until her end.

Ad.

7. *Tortured the thief who stole from Tiehmann,*
   Says, yes. Here it is a brief time, because of that she wanted to stand by it.

Ad.

8. *That the Evil Enemy went into Hans Köhler's leg according to her will, so that his leg wasted away,*
   Says, yes. With this she sighed and said: "Oh, if only it would come to an end, I am tired of it all here."

Ad.

9. *That according to her direction one of Til Schwartz's horses died,*

Says, yes.

Ad.

10. *That she put the things in a small pot in the name of the Devil on Jürgen Roleffes's farm, so that the said Roleffes should walk over it and become lame, how then through that he also got it in the head,*
    Says consistently, yes.

Ad.

11. *That through the Evil Enemy whispering to her she gave news to Autor Bahrensdorff where his lost horses and foals were,*
    Says, yes.

Ad.

12. *That on the bidding of her lover she carried a pot to a ditch where there was nice grass, where the cows of the current swineherd of Bechtsbüttel were grazing, from which one after the other died away,*
    Says, yes. She did that, with this, and with everything she had confessed before this, she wanted to stand consistently.

Ad.

13. *That she sent two things into the leg of the son of the same swineherd,*
    Says, yes, yes. She did not want to turn her words around, here it is temporal, but there it is eternal.

Ad.

14. *That she removed the things from Heinrich Cordes's bewitched child and sent them into Engelke Poppe's calf,*
    Says, yes. She did not want to turn her words around. Our Lord God should give her eternal happiness and blessedness, then she would be well looked after.

Post Examen[1]

Inquisitin says, she prayed many, many Lord's Prayers, and as you can see from her linen cap also cried bitterly today. She wished eternal blessedness and a joyful New Year for the E.E. Council and the court officers. The court officers had treated her well and had kept her well. She had had enough food and drink, more than she had sometimes wanted. God would repay it richly. But she would like to ask humbly and sadly, that the authorities would yet show her a mercy, to let her be beheaded, and to let her be buried in the earth. Should she be flogged, she would have to suffer that as well, the fire, the fire, /: *genuinatis verbis*[2] :/ that would be an eternal disgrace for her children, because of that would the authorities be merciful to her.

Also asked to have one hand loosened for a time, because both were locked up, so that /: *salva venia* :/ she could braid and clean her hair. She didn't want to kill herself, but stay consistently with God. Had she wanted to kill herself, it would have happened long ago.

---

1 "Following the examination."
2 "Her actual words."

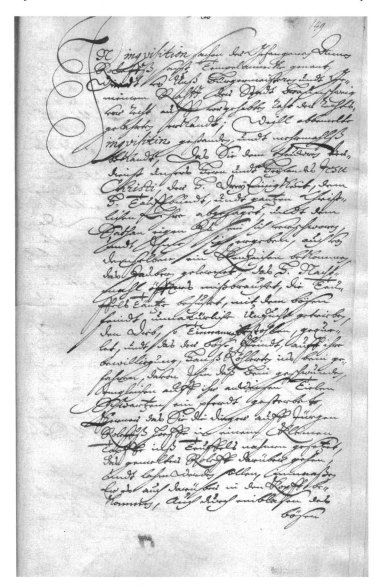

Figure 6 First page of Folio 44: The final judgment.

Figures 6 and 7 reproduce the two pages of Folio 44, the final judgment of the Higher Court, listing the charges of which Tempel Anneke was convicted and commuting her sentence to beheading. It is drafted and signed by the Syndicus, Johann Burchard Baumgarten of Hagen.

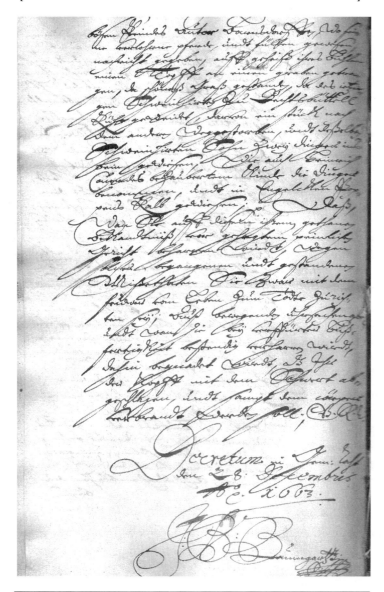

Figure 7 Second page of Folio 44: The final judgment.

Folio 44

[This is the final judgment of the Higher Court, based on Tempel Anneke's confession in Folio 43, drafted and signed by Johann Baumgarten.]

Judgment

Concerning the investigation of Anna Roleffes, otherwise called Tempel Anneke.

Concerning the investigation of the imprisoned Anna Roleffes, otherwise called Tempel Anneke, upon the received advice of the legal scholars, it is recognized as just by us, mayors and the General Council of the City of Brunswick, because the above mentioned *Inquisitin* admitted and confessed several times: that she renounced the Costly Sacrifice of our Lord and Saviour Jesus Christ, the H. Trinity, the H. Sacrament of Baptism, and the entire Christian doctrine, and swore to be Satan's own, and to submit to him, also she received a mark from the same, learned sorcery, often abused the H. Host, visited the Devil's dances, fornicated unnaturally with the Evil Enemy, tortured the thief who stole from Tiehmann, and that the Evil Enemy went into Hans Köhler's leg according to her will, so that his leg wasted away, in the same way according to her direction one of Til Schwartz's horses died. Further, she put the things in a small pot in the name of the Devil on Jürgen Roleffes's farm, so that the said Roleffes should walk over it and become lame, how then through that he also got it in the head. Also through the Evil Enemy whispering to her she gave news to Autor Bahrensdorff where his lost horses and foals were, on the bidding of her lover carried a pot to a ditch where there stood nice grass, where the cows of the current swineherd of Bechtsbüttel were grazing, from which one after the other died away, and she sent two things into the leg of the son of the same swineherd, how also she removed the things from Heinrich Cordes's bewitched child and sent them into Engelke Poppe's calf.

That, if she will persist in this her given confession before the supreme capital court, so because of the crimes committed and confessed to she will be condemned from life to death by fire. However, for previously mentioned reasons, and if she will consistently persist in her confession with felt penitence will be given mercy, in that her head will be cut off with a sword and shall be burned together with the body.

Decretum at the General Council,
the 28th *Decembris Anno* 1663
J. B. Baumgarten

Folio 45

[In accordance with the Carolina, a convicted criminal is required to make a last formal confession, called the *Urgicht*, on the day of the execution. This confession would have been read out at a public hearing just prior to the execution. See p. xxxiii of the Introduction.]

Urgicht[1]
by which Anna Roleffes of Harxbüttel stood consistently,
the 30th *Decembris Anno* 1663

---

1. Anna Roleffes of Harxbüttel, otherwise called Tempel Anneke, has admitted and several times confessed without torture, that she renounced the Costly Sacrifice of our Lord and Saviour Jesus Christ, the Holy Trinity, the Holy Sacrament of Baptism, and the entire Christian doctrine, and swore to be Satan's own, and to submit to him, upon that she received from Satan a mark on her body, and learned sorcery.

2. Further has Anna Roleffes admitted several times without torture, that she often abused the Holy Host, visited the Devil's or witches's dances, and fornicated unnaturally with the Evil Enemy.

3. In addition Anna Roleffes has several times admitted and confessed without torture, that she tortured the thief who stole from Hans Tiehmann, and that the Evil Enemy went into Hans Köhler's leg according to her will, so that from that it wasted away, in the same way according to her direction one of Til Schwartz's horses died.

4. Moreover Anna Roleffes has admitted without torture, that on Jürgen Roleffes's farm she put the things in a small pot in the name of the Devil, in order that the said Roleffes should walk over it and become lame, how then through that he also got it in the head.

5. Also Anna Roleffes has admitted and confessed without torture, that

---

1   Formal confession.

through the Evil Enemy whispering to her she divined for Autor Bahrensdorff where his lost horses and foals were. Then that on the bidding of her lover she carried a pot to a ditch where there stood nice grass, and where the cows of the current swineherd of Bechtsbüttel were grazing, from which one after the other died away.

6. Finally she also confessed several times and admitted without torture, that she sent two things into the leg of the son of the now mentioned swineherd, and that she had removed the things from Heinrich Cordes's bewitched child and sent them into Engelke Poppe's calf.

Anna Roleffes of Harxbüttel
otherwise called Tempel Anneke,
remaining consistently

The 30th *Decembris Anno* 1663

Supplementary Civic Records

[This section contains translations of additional archival documents related to the trial. For the background of these documents see pp. xxxvii-xxxviii of the Introduction.]

Record 1. Excerpt from the Civic Regulations (*Polizeiordnung*) of Brunswick, 17th Century, under "Z" for *Zauberei* (sorcery)[1]

3. Sorcery: Someone who damages another in his body or possessions through sorcery or poison shall without mercy be burned with fire to powder or be thrown on the wheel.

4. Someone who aims to help others or himself in their body, cattle or other goods with sorcery—if he is a stranger, he shall be banished from the city for a year, if he improved himself, he shall be given the entrance and exit again in exchange for a one mark fine—but if he is a citizen with property or a citizen's son, he shall be punished with a fine of three marks.

5. Someone who looks for reassurance, help, or advice from sorcerers or fortune-tellers shall pay 6 marks as a fine, and show himself willing to repent in front of the clergy, but a stranger shall be banished from the city for two years, and if he were to repent, regain entrance with a fine of two marks.

---

1   Brunswick City Archive B IV 13a Nr. 13, p. 32v.

Record 2. Court Salaries[1]

Administrative Salaries

Anno 1663	mr	β	d[2]
Dr. Georg Adam Struve Professor at Jena *Consiliarius*[3] received as his annual salary from this office	150	—	—
Dr. Johann Strauch *Syndicus*[4] received as his annual salary in the four quarters	360	—	—
Johann Burchard Baumgarten *Syndicus* received as his annual salary in the four quarters	360	—	—
Nicolaus Schomer *Consiliarius* received in the first quarter	60	—	—

Lower Court Magistrates, Scribes and Executioners Salary

Anno 1663	mr	β	d
Johann Velhagen, magistrate of Altstadt, received as his annual salary in the four quarters	60	—	—
Otto Theune, magistrate of Hagen, received as his annual salary in the four quarters	23	10	—
Johann Pilgram, court scribe, received as his annual salary	16	20	—
M. Hans Pfefferkorn, executioner, received as his annual salary	13	10	—
Summa hujus[5]	113	10	—

---

1   From Brunswick City Archive B II 1 182 (1663) *Der Stadt Braunschweig—Hauptrechnung De Anno M.DC. LXIII.*
2   For information about currency, see pp. xxxviii-xxxix.
3   "Judge." See p. xxxvi of the Introduction.
4   "Judge." See p. xxxvi of the Introduction.
5   Total of this.

Record 3. Excerpts from the Prisoner Accounts Books[1]

1663	mr	β	d
The 7th *Augustii*, to the bailiffs of Hagen, who had to ride to Gifhorn, Campen, and Neubrück concerning the incarcerated Tempel Anneke, as she was known, paid,[2]	—	16	6
The 18th *Octobris*, Hermann Mahner brought the judgment concerning Tempel Anneke from Jena, also the bailiff's salary, paid,	4	24	—
The 9th *Novembris* to the bailiff of Hagen who again carried letters concerning the imprisoned Tempel Anneke to Gifhorn and Neubrück, paid,	—	12	—
The 23rd *Decembris*, to the Law Faculty of Jena for a judgment concerning the imprisoned Tempel Anneke, and the messenger's wages, paid,	3	18	—
The 31st *Decembris* paid to Heinrich Graffenhorst, the bailiff in Hagen, for feeding the arrested for 196 days, *Item* capture and jail money, and what the officers of the court and magistrates, besides the executioner, consumed during *Territion*, the interrogations and the examinations, paid,	28	28	6

---

1   From Brunswick City Archive B II 1 182 (1663) *Der Stadt Braunschweig—Hauptrechnung De Anno M.DC. LXIII* pp. 58-63, and B II 1 183 (1664) *Der Stadt Braunschweig—Hauptrechnung De Anno M.DC.LXIV*, pp. 60-61.

2   This item is included in Rohmann (1983, p.6), but we were unable to find a record of it.

1664	mr	β	d

The 13th of January paid for a *Stübchen* of wine,
for the honourable Valentino Hesteler and the
honourable Hennig Dankwart,[1] who escorted
Tempel Anneke, beheaded and burned in the
past year, *ad locum supplicy*,[2] — 18 —

The 26th February for 2 *Stübchen* of {...}-wine,
2½ *Stübchen* of {...}-wine, ordered to be fetched
by mayor Henric van Adenstede,[3] 2¼ *Stübchen* of
Peter wine and 1½ Stübchen of Rhein wine
ordered to be fetched by mayor Christopher Berken,
while the condemned and burned witch,
Tempel Anneke, was executed, paid, 5 14 —

The 21st of April to master Hans Pfefferkorn, the
executioner, who beheaded and burned the executed
Tempel Anneke, also interrogated her several times
with and without torture before, paid,
according to the bill, 6 — —

---

1 Priests who accompanied Tempel Anneke to her execution.
2 To the place of execution.
3 A cloth merchant and senior mayor of the municipality of Altstadt.

Record 4. Testimony from the trial of Lücke Behrens for witchcraft, Brunswick 1672.[1]

[The following testimony from the trial of Lücke Behrens in 1672 describes the arrest of Tempel Anneke some nine years earlier. The testimony consists of answers by three witnesses to Question 22 of a Folio written on January 25, 1672. The testimony was followed by a deposition by Behrens' lawyer, responding to the three witness statements. According to these statements, Tempel Anneke was arrested at the house of a carpenter, Christian Loers, in Brunswick, who was later to be Behrens' second husband. Witnesses against Behrens claimed that she often had dealings with Tempel Anneke, although Behrens strongly denied any aquaintance with her.]

From the *Articulis defensionalis*: Questions put forward in the defence of the innocent Lücke Behrens, wife of Christian Loers. January 25, 1672.

22.   *Item* is it true that the witness never saw Tempel Anneke come from the house of the imprisoned?

January 31, 1672.
Andreas Dunsten testifies
Ad 22
Says never, except when the same[2] was arrested, for she was said to have drunk brandy at the *Hoppschen* house[3] and the Chief Magistrate together with the guards took her out of the *Hoppschen* house.

January 31, 1672.
Hans Dunsten testifies
Ad 22
He did not see it, but the word going around was that the guards took her from the house, and there was talk that she drank brandy there.

---

1   From Brunswick City Archive C V 101: 133r, 149v, 150v, 157r, 172r.
2   Tempel Anneke.
3   Here the witness is referring to Lücke Behrens by her first husband's name, Julius Hoppe. At the time of Tempel Anneke's arrest the house belonged to Behrens's future second husband, Christian Loers. Behrens did not live in that house at the time of Tempel Anneke's arrest.

February 5, 1672.
Hans Riechelmann, carpenter, testifies
Ad 22
He never saw Tempel Anneke except when the guards took her into custody in front of the door of Christian Loers, current husband of the imprisoned.

March 21, 1772.
From the deposition of Dietrich Heinrich Rasch, lawyer for Lücke Behrens

... the reason, however, that she[1] came with her son to the husband of the *Inquisitin*[2] was that he was to build a house in Harxbüttel for her[3] son, at the request of H. Mandelsow, as the magistrate of the bishopric of St. Blasius.

---

1 Tempel Anneke.
2 Christian Loers.
3 Tempel Anneke's. Christian Loers was a carpenter, and as such was apparently hired by the bishopric to build a house for Tempel Anneke's son. We do not know the circumstances of this arrangement, except that the bishopric owned the land on which Tempel Anneke's son's farm was located.

Appendices

Appendix A. Glossary of Latin Terms

We have included here the most frequently occuring Latin terms. Those that occur only once are translated in foootnotes. Some abbreviations and word endings are not listed here.

Word or Phrase	Specific Occurances	Translation
Actus, also Act., Actum		legal proceeding
	Num. Actor. (Numero Actorum) …	proceeding number …
	in Actis. Num. …; *Act. Num.* …	in proceeding number …
	Actum ut Supra	the proceeding as above
	sub Num Actorum (Actor.) …	under proceeding number …
ad		to; with respect to
	ad acta	with respect to the proceedings, for the legal record
	ad … *Artm. (Articulum)*	with respect to article …
	ad Artm. (ad Articulum)	with respect to the article
	ad Artos. (ad articulos)	with respect to the articles
	ad hunc Artm. (Articulum)	with respect to this article
	ad proxe praecedentem Inquisitionalem	with respect to the preceding investigation
	ad proxe praecedentem Artm.	with respect to the preceding article
Addit.		additional
admonita / us de veritate dicenda		she/he was warned that she/he must tell the truth

Word or Phrase	Specific Occurances	Translation
Anno		in the year
Articulo; also Artm. Articul. (Articulum)	*Articulos / Articuli Inquisitionalis*	article of speech or text; in this case a question or statement from the record investigational article/s
captiva		prisoner in custody (feminine)
carnificus	*in praesentia carnificis*	executioner in the presence of the executioner
Cessat		remains silent
Cessat Confrontatio		end of the confrontation
Confrontatio		confrontation [with witnesses]
decretum, decreto		decree
formalibus verbis		using the proper words
gravia admonita de evitando perjuro ejusq. atrocissima poena		with a strong warning about avoiding perjury and its severe penalty
gravia de veritate dicenda admonitione,		with a strong warning about saying the truth
gravia admonitione de veritate dicenda		
in praesentia		in the presence of
in silentium		solemnly
in specie		in appearance or pretence
Inquisitin (feminine)		the accused or investigated

Word or Phrase	Specific Occurances	Translation
Inquisition		investigation
	Inquisition Actis / Acte	investigation proceeding/s
	inquisitional	of the investigation
	Inquisitional Articulos (Articul.)	investigation questions
instrumentum / a		instrument/s
interrogatio / atoria		question/s
item		also, likewise
justitio		justice
Justitio		institution of justice
N.N. (Nomen Nescio)		I am ignorant of the name
negat iterum		denied again
Nota		Note
protocollo, protocollum		record
	ex protocollo	from the record
	extract protocolli	extract from the record
ratione confrontationis		record of the confrontation
Requisitoriales (Requisitorialibus)		request
	Requisitoriales in subsid. (subsidium juris)	request in the service of justice
salva venia		I beg your pardon

Word or Phrase	Specific Occurances	Translation
subsidium	*subsidial; subsidiarisch* *in subsidium, subsidiaris* *in subsidium juris*	aid, help, support subsidial; supporting in the aid of (the purpose) in the aid of justice
Territion		the showing and demonstration of torture instruments, as opposed to the actual applica- tion of torture
testis		witness

Figure 8 Christmas Rose (*helleborus niger*). This is an engraving of a Christmas Rose, one of the herbs used by Tempel Anneke and mentioned by Laurentius Gieseler in Folio 23.

Appendix B. Index of Herbs and Medicinal Ingredients

English	German	Botanical	Folio Numbers
aloe	aloe	Aloe	aloe vera 20
angelica	Angelika (Engelwurtzel)	angelica archangelica	22, 23, 26
ashes	Asche		18
beer	Bier		22
blackberry	Brombeere (Brampte, Bremete)	rubus fructicosus	18, 26
boar lard	Borch-Schwein Schmalz		3
brookweed	Bunge	samolus valerandi	18
buckthorn	Kreuzdorn	rhamnus catharticus	3
calf ashes	Asche vom Kalb		3
carline thistle	Eberwurzel	carlina vulgaris	22, 23
chalk	Kreide		20, 26
chervil	Kerbel	anthriscus cerefolium	7, 22, 23
chicory	Zichorie (Cikorwurtzel)	cichorium intybus	3
christmas rose	Christrose (Christwurtz)	helleborus niger	3, 20, 23
cow manure	Kuhmist		6
egg	Ei		22
elderberry	Holunder (Alhorn)	Sambucus	28
flax	Leinen, Flachs	linum usitatissimum	22, 23
hops	Feldhopfen, Holzhopfen	humulus lupulus	3, 18, 26

English	German	Botanical	Folio Numbers
juniper berry	Wachholderbeeren	juniperus communis	3
linseed	Leinsamen		22, 23
lungwort	Lungenkraut (Lungenwort)	sticta pulmonaria	3, 26
mandrake	Alraune (Alrünecken)	atropa mandragora	B, 20, 21, 22
milk	Milch		26
oak leaves	Eichen Laub	quercus robur	18
peacock feathers	Pfauenfedern (Pagelnußfedern)		22, 23
resin	Harz		3
rue	Raute	ruta graveolens	6, 26
rye	Roggen		18
saffron	Safran	crocus sativus	20, 26
salt	Salz		18, 26
sheep ashes	Asche vom Schaf		18, 26, 27
stork's dung	Storch- oder Heilbartsdreck	stercus ciconiae	23
stork's oil	Storchöl	olium ciconiae	22, 23
turnip-rooted chervil	Kälberkropf	chaerophyllum bulbosum	28
vinegar	Essig		6
watercress	Brunnenkresse (Bornkresse)	nasturtium officinale	3
wax	Wachs		3
wild sage	Wildes Salbei	salvia officinalis	3, 18, 26

English	German	Botanical	Folio Numbers
wine	Wein		3
wormwood	Beifuß (Vermuth)	artemisia campestris	26
yellow iris (possibly)	Heilbartsklappern	iris pseudacorus (possibly)	22, 23
unknown	Allard-, Schwerdteienwurtzel		22
unknown	Ballei		22, 23
unknown	heerößel		7

References

Ankarloo, B. and Clark, S. (Eds.) (2001). *Witchcraft and Magic in Europe: The Middle Ages*. London: Athlone Press.

———. (Eds.) (2002). *Witchcraft and Magic in Europe: The Period of the Witch Trials*. London: Athlone Press.

Ankarloo, B. (2002). "Witch-Trials in Northern Europe, 1450–1700." In Ankarloo and Clark (2002): 53–95.

Behringer, W. (1997). *Witchcraft Persecutions in Bavaria: Popular Magic, Religious Zealotry and Reason of State in Early Modern Europe*. Ed. and trans. J.C. Grayson and D. Lederer. Cambridge: Cambridge University Press. (This is a translation of *Hexenverfolgung in Bayern: Volksmagie, Glaubenseifer, und Staatsräson in der Frühen Neuzeit*. Munich, 1987.)

Bodin, J. (1580/2001). *On the Demon-Mania of Witches*. Ed., trans., and abridged R.A. Scott and J.L. Pearl. Toronto: Centre for Reformation and Renaissance Studies. (This is a translation of *De la démonomanie des sorciers*. Paris, 1580.)

Briggs, R. (1996). *Witches and Neighbours: The Social and Cultural Context of European Witchcraft*. London: HarperCollins.

Clark, S. (1991). "The Rational Witchfinder: Conscience, Demonological Naturalism and Popular Superstitions." In S. Pumfrey, P.L Rossie, and M. Slawinski, eds. *Science, Culture and Popular Belief in Renaissance Europe*. Manchester: Manchester University Press: 222–48.

———. (1997). *Thinking with Demons: The Idea of Witchcraft in Early Modern Europe*. Oxford: Oxford University Press.

———. (2002). "Witchcraft and Magic in Early Modern Culture." In Ankarloo and Clark (2002): 97–169.

Cohn, N. (1993). *Europe's Inner Demons: The Demonization of Christians in Medieval Christendom*. 2nd ed. Chicago: University of Chicago Press.

Deutsches Rechtswörterbuch: Wörterbuch der älteren deutschen (westgermanischen) Rechtssprache. Forschungsstelle der Heidelberger Akademie der Wissenschaften http://www.rzuser.uni-heidelberg.de/. Retrieved April 2005 (website last updated 15 February 2005).

Deutsches Wörterbuch von Jacob und Wilhelm Grimm auf CD-ROM und im Internet. DFG-Projekt im Fach Germanistik der Universität Trier. http://germ83.uni-trier.de/DWB. Retrieved April 2005 (website last updated 6 October 2003).

Görges, W. and Spehr, F. (1892) *Geschichten und Sagen von Stadt und Land Braunschweig*. Braunschweig: Archiv-Verlag.

Heinrich Julius, Duke of Brunswick-Wolfenbüttel (1593). *Constitution wornach sich das Consistorium auch die Prediger mit der Kirchen Disciplin verhalten sollen.* Reprinted in *Ausführlicher Wahrhaffter Historischer Bericht / die Fürstliche Land- und Erbstadt Braunschweig, Auch der Herzogen zu Braunschweig und Lüneburg Wolfenbüttelschen Theils darüber habende Landesfürstliche Hoch: Obrig und Gerechtigkeit, auch ihre der Stadt unmittelbare angeborne schüldige Subiection und Unterthenigkeit ... betreffend.* Helmstedt: Lucius, 1607. Vol. 2: 60-62

Jarck, H.R. and Schildt, G. (Eds.) (2000). *Die Braunschweigische Landesgeschichte: Jahrtausendrückblick einer Region*. Brunswick: Appelhans.

Jolly, K.L. (2001). "Medieval Magic: Definitions, Beliefs, and Practices." In Ankarloo and Clark (2001): 1-71.

Kauertz, C. (2001). *Wissenschaft und Hexenglaube: Die Diskussion des Zauber- und Hexenwesens an der Universität Helmstedt (1576–1620)*. Bielefeld: Verlag für Regionalgeschichte.

Kors, A. and Peters E. (Eds.) (2001). *Witchcraft in Europe 1400–1700*. 2nd ed. Philadelphia: University of Pennsylvania Press.

Kieckhefer, R. (1976). *European Witch Trials: Their Foundations in Popular and Learned Culture*. Berkeley: University of California Press

———. (1989). *Magic in the Middle Ages*. Cambridge: Cambridge University Press.

Kunze, M. (1987). *Highroad to the Stake: A Tale of Witchcraft*. Trans. W.E. Yuill. Chicago: University of Chicago Press.

Langbein, J.L. (1974). *Prosecuting Crime in the Renaissance: England, Germany and France*. Cambridge, MA: Harvard University Press.

Lehrmann, J. (1997). *Hexen- und Dämonenglaube im Lande Braunschweig: Die Geschichte einer Verfolgung unter regionalem Aspekt*. Lehrte: Lehrmann-Verlag.

Levack, B. (1995). *The Witch-Hunt in Early Modern Europe*. 2nd ed. London: Longman.

———. (Ed.) (2001). *New Perspectives on Witchcraft, Magic and Demonology*. 6 vols. London: Routledge.

Lexer, M. (1885/1992). *Mittelhochdeutsches Taschenwörterbuch*. 3rd Ed. Stuttgart: Hirzel.

Lübben, A. (1888/1995). *Mittelniederdeutsches Handwörterbuch*. Darmstadt: Wissenschaftliche Buchgesellschaft.

Midelfort, E.H.C. (1972). *Witch Hunting in Southwestern Germany 1562–1684: The Social and Intellectual Foundations*. Stanford: Stanford University Press.

Monderhack, R. (1997). *Braunschweiger Stadtgeschichte*. Brunswick: Waisenhaus.

Monter, W. (2002). "Witch-Trials in Continental Europe, 1560–1660." In Ankarloo and Clark (2002): 1–52.

Peters, E. (2001). "The Medieval Church and State on Superstition, Magic, and Witchcraft from Augustine to the Sixteenth Century." In Ankarloo and Clark (2001): 173-245.

Rehtmeier, J. and Bünting, H. (1722). *Braunschweig-Lüneburgische Chronic, Oder: Historische Beschreibung der Herzöge zu Braunschweig und Lüneburg*. 3 vols. Braunschweig: Detleffsen.

Rhamm, U. (1882). *Hexenglaube und Hexenprocesse vornämlich in den braunschweigischen Landen*. Wolfenbüttel: Julius Zwißler.

Rohmann, K. (1983). *Tempel-Anneke: Der Prozeß gegen die letzte "Hexe" von Braunschweig 1663*. Hildesheim: August Lax.

Roper, L. (1994). *Oedipus and the Devil: Witchcraft, Sexuality and Religion in Early Modern Europe*. New York: Routledge.

———. (2004). *Witch Craze: Terror and Fantasy in Baroque Germany*. New Haven: Yale University Press.

Rowlands, A. (2001). "Witchcraft and Old Women in Early Modern Germany." *Past & Present* 173: 50–89.

———. (2003). *Witchccraft Narratives in Germany: Rothenburg, 1561-1652*. Manchester: Manchester University Press.

Schormann, G. (1977). *Hexenprozesse in Nordwest Deutschland*. Hildesheim: August Lax.

Schroeder, F.-C. (Ed.) (2000). *Die Peinliche Gerichtsordnung Kaiser Karls V. und des Heiligen Römischen Reichs*. Stuttgart: Philipp Reclam. Originally published 1532.

Schütte, Otto. (1907). Zauberei in Braunschweig im 16. und 17. *Braunschweigisches Magazin* 12: 134–38.

Spiess, W. (1954). Die Gerichtsverfassung der Stadt Braunschweig zur Hansezeit. In W. Spiess, ed., *Beiträge zur Geschichte des Gerichtswesens im Lande Braunschweig*. Brunswick: Waisenhaus: 39–77.

———. (1966). *Geschichte der Stadt Braunschweig im Nachmittelalter: Vom Ausgang des Mittelalters bis zum Ende der Stadtfreiheit (1491–1671)*. 2 vols. Brunswick: Waisenhaus.

———. (1970). Die Ratsherren der Hansestadt Braunschweig 1231–1671. Brunswick: Waisenhaus.

Summers, M. (1928.) (Trans. and ed.) *The Malleus Maleficarum of Heinrich Kramer and Jacob Sprenger*. London. Reprinted by Dover Press, 1971. This is a translation of H. Kramer, *Malleus Maleficarum*, first published Speyer: Peter Drach 1487.

Thomas, K. (1971) *Religion and the Decline of Magic: Studies in Popular Beliefs in Sixteenth and Seventeenth Century England*. London: Weidenfeld and Nicolson.

Trevor-Roper, H. (1967). "The European Witch-Craze of the Sixteenth and Seventeenth Centuries." In H. Trevor-Roper, *Religion, the Reformation and Social Change and other Essays*. Reprinted in *The European Witch-Craze of the Sixteenth and Seventeenth Centuries and Other Essays*. New York: Harper & Row, 1969.

Wrampelmeyer. (1910). Der letßte Hexenprozeß in der Stadt Braunschweig. *Hannoverland 4*, 218–21.

Sources

We gratefully acknowledge permission from the *Stadtarchiv Braunschweig* to reproduce Figures 4, 5, 6, 7, and Map 3.

Actum in der Fronerey im Hagen, 7.8.1663, *Vorderseite* (*Stadtarchiv Braunschweig* H V: 250, Blatt 43 r),

Medicinisches Gutachten Dr. Laurentius Gieseler, 27.8.1663, (*Stadtarchiv Braunschweig* H V: 250, Blatt 88 r),

Urteil J. B. Baumgarten, 28.12.1663 (*Stadtarchiv Braunschweig* H V: 250, Blatt 149 r), and Map 3 (*Stadtarchiv Braunschweig* H XI 93: 3.)

We gratefully acknowledge permission from the *Braunschweig Landesmuseum* to reproduce Maps 1 and 2 *"Plan der Stadt Braunschweig von 1671"* (Inv.-Nr. LMB 31493), Figures 1 and 3 *"Ansicht von Braunschweig von Osten. Merian nach Conrad Buno, 1641"* (Inv.-Nr.: 1313), and Figure 5 *"Beck – Ansicht Opernhaus"* (Inv.-Nr.: LMB 30658.)

For the photographic reproduction of Maps 1 and 2, and Figures 1, 2, and 3, we thank *Repro Braunschweigisches Landesmuseum,* I. Simon.

Index of People and Places

Number indicates folio number. Place names are in bold